I0517693

Open Your Heart

Ruth Cherry Ph. D.

EXPLORA BOOKS
700–838 West Hastings St. Vancouver, BC V6C 0A6
www.explorabooks.com
Phone: (604) 330 6795

No part of this book may be reproduced, stored in a retrieval system, or transmitted by any means without the written permission of the author.

Because of the dynamic nature of the Internet, any web addresses or links contained in this book may have changed since publication and may no longer be valid. The views expressed in this work are solely those of the author and do not necessarily reflect the views of the publisher, and the publisher hereby disclaims any responsibility for them.

ISBN: 978-1-998394-50-0

© 2024 Ruth Cherry Ph. D. All rights reserved

Ruth Cherry, Ph.D

OPEN YOUR HEART

Books authored by Ruth Cherry, Ph.D.

Living in the Flow
Practicing Vibrational Alignment

Accepting Unconditional Love
An Introspective Journey to A New and Vibrant Relationship with Source

Transformation Workbook Matters of the Heart
Defer to a wisdom greater than your mind's.

Matters of the Soul

Table of Contents

CHAPTER 1
HANNAH

It's Sunday night and I'm returning home, beat and starving. My keys slip into the two deadbolt locks as I balance a stack of books on my hip. My head pounds and I'm generally annoyed. It's been a frustrating day.

The table by the door catches my keys and my gloves. I glance in the mirror above it quickly and notice that my nose and cheeks are chilled pink and my short brown hair is mussed. Some women do carefree well; I don't.

Out of habit, I align the books I've just set down with the edge of the table. I notice some lint on the carpet and deposit it in my pocket. I walk into the kitchen to the left of the entry hall, glad that I did my whirlwind cleaning this morning.

Hoping to erase the winter chill which lingers in my bones, I turn the heat on High under the tea kettle. Then I race for the bathroom. Three minutes later with my pantyhose around one ankle, I hobble back to the shrieking tea kettle which apparently was not as full as I had thought. Steam billows over the stove and my glasses fog. I pull them off, lay them on the table, and grab the tea kettle.

As I pour the hot water into my cup on the counter I freeze.

Did I really see what I thought I saw? I look back at the table. An old woman sits there smoking! My first thought is that I don't own an ashtray and I don't allow anyone to smoke in my condo. What is she doing?!

And then I realize THERE IS AN INTRUDER IN MY HOME! WHO IS SHE AND HOW DID SHE GET IN HERE?

She looks to be a plump, frazzled homemaker. Apparently, she's been cooking; her apron is stained with tomato sauce and there are beads of perspiration at her hairline.

She's leaning over the kitchen table, elbows bent, the ash on her cigarette an inch long. Her frizzy brown hair is pinned up in the back and she says, "Anne, you gotta minute? We need to talk." She's Jewish? Or Italian? She's some ethnicity that I am not.

And I jerk back to attention. WHAT IS GOING ON?

She continues, "I'm a surprise, huh? You expected maybe an angel and instead, it's just me, Hannah, in the kitchen."

I don't know what she's talking about but before I can say that she interjects, "It's OK. I'm not made to order. I am definitely not your fantasy guide floating above it all."

She laughs and snorts a bit and then coughs. Her voice is coarse as it passes through a sandpaper throat. Her cough sounds like the sandpaper is being torn and rubbed against itself. With her coughs assaulting me I find myself leaning away from her.

She blows her nose into a rumpled handkerchief which she stuffs in a side pocket of her apron. Her yellow nicotine-stained fingers backdrop her ragged nails, outlined by tomato sauce. I feel like a voyeur, watching another human go about the everyday private acts of being a person.

I'm over my initial consternation and now I'm curious. And embarrassed. Mostly for her. I have worked to develop a polished appearance and would never let myself be seen in this state. I want to protect her from my seeing but I remind myself that SHE'S IN MY KITCHEN!

"Who are you and why are you sitting in my home?"

Hannah has recovered from her coughing fit by drinking some water. A drop hangs at the corner of her mouth. "I've come because you called for me. I know I'm not what you were looking for. I'm not someone to show off. I won't help you impress anyone. But what I know is something you don't and you don't even know you're missing it."

I called for her? When?

"What are you talking about?" And immediately I wonder why I'm talking to her at all. "Hannah ..." She interrupts me to answer my unspoken thought.

"When you prayed. You called for me when you prayed." When I prayed? I don't pray. What IS she talking about?

"You know, when you said, 'Good God, what am I doing wrong?' and 'Jesus Christ, why is life so hard?' You know, those prayers." She inhales deeply and blows smoke toward the ceiling.

I had said those things. More than a few times lately. I've been very frustrated.

"So, that's why I'm here. Because of you." She rummages through her apron pocket, dropping some change on the floor.

All my life I've appreciated refinement, a tasteful low-key subtlety.

Hannah is not that.

"Please tell me again what this is all about," I stammer, trying to make sense of this seemingly nonsensical situation. I'm willing to be reasonable. If she has come to me because of my "prayers," I'll listen. But that's all. I am definitely not impressed. She wants to talk? Let her talk.

"OK, I will." Again, she answers my thought but her attention is only on her words and her cigarette. As she rolls her cigarette between her thumb and her forefinger, she doesn't look at me. "You see, what you've done, well, I don't know that I would have done it that way, but OK, Anne, you have, so let's start from here. What you've done is to put your spirituality all in your head. You use it to get away from your life. A bit screwy to my way of thinking, but now you're here and we're talking and we'll just take it from this point."

Articulate she's not.

Hannah acknowledges my unvoiced comment. "I told you I don't fit your image of what a teacher should be. Now, I'm getting tired of your impertinence, so you just listen to me and quit crowding my mind with your thoughts. OK, so here is where we are. You're 45, right? And your life is OK but you've completely lost me."

I try not to laugh. Does she think I've been looking for her? Oh no, she's already felt my disdain. While I don't respect her, I don't need to insult her, either.

She's losing her sense of humor. "Will you listen?! I know it offends your dignity to realize that I'm your teacher but I'm the part of you that you have never developed and the part of you that you don't know. I'm ordinary and every day and I take care of little chores. I haven't accomplished anything big and I don't want to. I feel pretty good about being down here on the ground and taking care of my little bitty concerns."

She glances at me. I'm staring at my cuticles. Seeing hers reminds me to schedule a manicure.

"Will you listen to me?!!" she demands more than asks.

I find her annoying. I'm sure she is a fine person and all, but, really, I'm not too keen about sitting here with her. And she knows that.

"Listen, sweetheart," she continues, "I didn't volunteer for this job. I don't want to be here. I have other things I could be doing."

I laugh out loud now and say, "I'm sorry, I just don't understand who you are or why you're here or what you want me to know."

"For being so smart you're pretty dumb." And she fiddles with her cigarette. I hate smoking.

I look down at my lap and I shiver. I tell myself this is not happening. But when I look up, she's still in front of me.

"Hannah, thanks for dropping by but . . ."

"Not so fast. You're not the one in charge here. You've always thought you could be in control and you thought you could make your life look just the way you wanted it to, but. . ." and another coughing fit overtakes her. I offer her the glass of water with tomato fingerprints on it. I wipe my hands after I pass it to her.

"See? That is so much like you. You don't want to get your fingers dirty."

I protest, "I was just . . ."

"Be quiet!" she booms and I'm taken aback by the violence of her response. "You are always trying to get away from what is real. You think too much."

WHO IS THIS PERSON?

"Are you real or are you part of my fantasy world that you're so critical of?" I ask. I hope she notices that I ended that sentence with a preposition, trying not to be too perfect.

Hannah gets up from the table and walks to the sink and brushes something off her apron. "I'm not sure you're ready to hear me just yet. You still think you can do life from your head. You still want to be in control. Well, I have nothing to say to you until you lose that piece of gibberish." And she turns her back to me and runs water in the sink.

I'm tempted to walk away. After all, this is just a figment of my imagination. She's just in my head. But Hannah hears that thought, too.

"No, dear, I am not just in your head. Not in the way your other mind creations are just in your head." And she mimics my judgment. She tilts her head back and lifts her nose in the air. She forces her words through her tight lips. I don't like being made fun of.

"So what, you don't like it," Hannah dares me to complain.

I am really annoyed with my lack of privacy. Since when are my thoughts not my own?

"Since right now, dearie, and get used to it, 'cause you're never going back to being your little uptight super-independent I-can-do-it-myself figurine of a human. Never. Get it? Times have changed. Wake up and smell the . . ." And her voice trails off.

"Coffee," I offer derisively. "Or maybe roses." I find myself tidying up her conversation by finishing her sentence. I like things neat.

"Hmm? Yeah, yeah, whatever. I'm here because you have been praying so hard and so loud. I swear sometimes your voice is deafening. It pounds in my head. Baboom . . . baboom . . . bababoom . . . 'Good God, I wish this craziness would end' . . . baboom . . . 'Jesus Christ, stop the world'. . . baboom . . . 'God in heaven, help me.' Well, please GOD, I'm here now and you don't even want to listen to me! You're a hypocrite; do you know that? That's what you are. A prissy little know-it-all hypocrite. So, don't listen to me. I don't care. I'll go back to where I was. I don't need you.

You need me. But if you think you don't, well, that's OK. Keep doing your life your way. Just save yourself some time and stop with the babooms. They're giving me a headache."

Now Hannah has my attention. It's true. I have been complaining; I wouldn't call it praying. Life is not at all the way I expected it to be. By this time in my 40's I thought I would be settled and be normal and finally fit in.

I thought all those insecurities from my teen years and my 20s would have disappeared. Instead, they evolved to a more complex life form. Now I don't worry about dates (or no dates), I worry that I'm not doing life right. I don't question if others think I'm OK, I'm more concerned that I don't really like myself. I no longer worry about establishing myself in my profession, but I wonder if I'll ever truly be happy.

I've done everything right but still, just as Hannah says, there is something escaping me. There is something about being alive that I'm just not getting. That's what my question, frustration and my complaining (in her words "praying") have been about.

And, apparently, Hannah is my answer. I can't very well turn away from her if she's come to me when I've asked for direction. So, immediately, and maybe a bit insincerely, I shift my tone to conciliatory.

"Thank you very much for coming, Hannah. I appreciate your attention."

She looks at me sideways from her place at the sink. "Don't talk down to me. I don't care how your life goes. And if you don't, well, then there's no problem." She harrumphs. I've never known anyone with such a repertoire of expressive vocalizations.

I want to reassure her. "Oh, but I do care about my life. I truly want something more but I thought it would come in an insight when I meditate that would reveal the Universe to me or a friendship with just the right person, someone who truly understands me and appreciates me or . . ." I can almost feel myself levitate.

Hannah barges into my reverie. "Forget it. You're on the wrong track. You're not even looking in the right direction so how can you hope to see what you're looking for? You still think that you know. But, toots, you know nothing. And when you're ready to accept that, we can talk. Until then you're just spinning your wheels and pretending that you're alive. But you're not. Being alive is such a gift and you're frittering your time away." She ends with a snort. She seems pretty self-righteous if you ask me, which she didn't.

If I had read her words on paper I would have been magnetized. Seeing her in person, I have trouble taking her seriously. Her profound statements and her sloppy appearance pull my mind in different directions. I want her wisdom but I don't really like her.

So, I respond equally self-righteously. "What do you mean? I am responsible. I exercise every day or almost every day. I meditate and I write in my journal. I'm not unkind to anyone . . . well, unless they really annoy me and then they deserve it. I recycle and I even do volunteer work. How can you tell me I'm not doing life right?"

I am steamed. Gratuitous criticism from someone I'm pretty sure is a fantasy. And a messy fantasy at that. I don't have to be passive and take this.

"It wouldn't hurt you to be passive," Hannah replies, invading my thought-space even though I've attempted to establish my boundary around it. "No, it wouldn't hurt you one bit. You think you know so much but you are so lost." And she rolls her eyes.

Then Hannah dries her hands and sits back down at the table. In a softer voice, she continues as she peers into my eyes.

"Anne, you gotta stop. Stop trying so hard. Stop working so much. You work at everything. You even work at playing. Just stop it. Will you sit back and take it easy and trust? Trust that your life will be OK if you're not pushing your way through every little thing that comes up, using your mind like a steam roller? Trust that things will turn out just fine without your trying to control every move?"

She is soothing now and I'm touched. Her words pierce the fear that has always lived inside me. The fear that's hiding behind my abundant anxiety. The fear that if I don't take care of myself, no one else will. Hannah has entered my heart with her gentleness.

I cry softly and that surprises me. Usually, I don't like people to see my unprotected side but Hannah isn't really a person. Not a separate person.

"That's right, dear," Hannah whispers. "I already know you better than you know yourself. There isn't anything you could hide from me if you tried. Your fear is what's underneath all this rushing around. And beneath your seriousness. And behind your thinking."

Now I want to talk to her. I want to tell her about what I fear — the loneliness and the depressions — but she shushes me. "I already know. Life has been hard but it doesn't have to be hard any longer. Not if you make some different choices."

Immediately, I perk up. Now she's speaking my language.

There is something I can do. I always knew it. Now I can make things turn out right. Hannah is the informant with the magic message I've been waiting for.

"I'll do it. Just tell me what it is," I gush in my eagerness to own the life-fulfilling secret. "I won't hold back."

"That's wonderful, dear. What I want you to do is open your heart and surrender to life. That's all. OK?"

OK? OK, to what? Open my heart? Surrender to life? These words sound great but what do they mean?

"Hannah, I thought we were getting somewhere but now I don't know. I'll do anything you tell me but what does 'surrender to life' mean? You want me to stay in bed all day? That's passive. You want me to forget my work? What?" My temporary hope for receiving specific life instructions is frustrated by her vagueness. Now I want her to be concrete.

She is silent for a moment as she studies the tabletop.

"I want you to forget everything you know. I want you to listen to me. I want you to take me with you everywhere you go. I am with you already — I just want you to realize that and to ask me when you need to make a decision. I want you to trust me."

Trust is not my long suit and I bet she knows that. I much prefer self-reliance and independence. That's how I've always managed to get by. But for some incomprehensible reason, what has worked for me in the past is just not working anymore. No matter how hard I try, I can't force my life to fit the form I prefer.

At this point, I desperately need a change. The frustration grows daily and I'm more and more unhappy. I can't continue the way I've been going but I don't know what to do differently. I need something new, but what?

So, if Hannah is the answer to some pretty powerful "praying" and if she has something to give me, I have an opening I haven't seen before. As yet I'm not certain what this "opportunity" is, but I have no alternatives. Out of desperation and with no other apparent choices at this stage of my life, I commit to her.

"You got it, Hannah. I'm yours." I am pleased with my final decision to participate in this adventure with her, conveniently overlooking my intense resistance up to this point.

"Yeah, we'll see."

CHAPTER 2
THE CONTROLLER

The next morning, Monday, I woke 15 minutes earlier than usual. I allocate the extra time to spend with Hannah before I leave for a day filled with appointments. I am ready to initiate the new plan for happiness which I am sure she is promising me.

After I dress with my briefcase packed and waiting for me near the door, I sit in the overstuffed blue chair in my living room. It hugs me when I lean back in it.

"OK, Hannah," and I close my eyes, "I'm ready for you to come to me. Tell me what to do today." And I wait.

Another five minutes. "I'm here. Whatever you want to say, I'm listening." Still . . . nothing. A few more minutes and the time I had allotted is gone. "Tonight," I think. "I'll have more time tonight." And I race out the door, throw my briefcase in the passenger seat of my old but trusty Honda, and enter the freeway for the usual forty-minute drive to my office.

I had opened my private practice office to do psychotherapy when I received my license as a psychologist. After graduate school, I chose private practice for the flexibility and the freedom it afforded. I could decide where I would work, when, and with whom. Private practice also allowed me the opportunity to see clients for less than most agencies charge. I like working with people who are motivated even if they can't afford the usual therapy fee. And I'm not a team player. I do things my way.

Practicing psychotherapy was not quite what I had expected. In school, I had read transcripts of Carl Rogers' sessions and I was ready to imitate him. I could say, "Yes, yes, Hmmm . . ." or "Hmmm? (with a slight head nod) . . ." or "I understand." I perfected accurate empathy and precise reflection of the client's feelings. I was so good at being present that I impressed myself.

After my first month in practice, I had to wonder where Carl had found his bright, self-aware, compliant clients. From the community networking I had done in Hanover, the small town in which I opened my office, I received referrals — young mothers who couldn't manage their children, middle-aged wives who had been angry for years but were only now recognizing it, a few alcoholics, and couples who were surprised to find that their mate was not the person they thought they had married. Regular folks struggling to live regular lives.

It was good work, perfect for me even with the adjustments I had to make in my expectations. I felt privileged to be involved in others' growth. Sessions that were healing for them healed me, also. I lived vicariously, I admit it, and I loved my work life.

I was in practice for twenty years and I learned a tremendous amount. I saw how my conflicts were reflected to me by my clients. They said words that echoed my feelings. What I couldn't resolve, they didn't either. When I did get my craziness worked out, they sailed past their obstacles.

I was benefitting personally from doing therapy in addition to being paid. Too good to be true. (I hoped it was as valuable for the clients.) For twenty years my work was my life and my life was my work.

But these last six months I've felt restless. For two decades, I thought about other people and tried to help them but now something inside me pulls me away from them and into myself. I feel a growing impatience doing the same thing over and over whereas a few months ago, the routine was comforting. The clients are still fine and I actually am a better therapist than ever (having added a few skills over the years), but I want something more. I feel frustrated and vaguely dissatisfied even though I can't identify a specific problem. I just know that something has to change.

Hannah is not the change I hoped for but her appearance is intriguing. I don't understand her thought process, but she is new and I am ready for something different. I'm disappointed that I didn't see her this morning. After fighting her so hard initially, I allow for the possibility that she just might say something I need to hear.

In my business suit and my worker mentality, I slam the door on the Hannah experience and I drive to work. My drive is the same as it always is. After twenty years of driving this road daily, I have it memorized. Only if I need to change my routine do I get into trouble. My car and I are on auto pilot and we resist detours.

The Southern California freeway rushes through one small town indistinguishable from the next. Every few miles the name of the town I drive through is announced by a small white sign with a poppy in the corner — Salida follows Glenwood follows Northrop follows Axelrod follows Longdale, etc. There is no end to the shopping centers along the freeway and no variance in their appearance. For a girl from the Midwest, this consumer uniformity erases any personality the individual towns might offer. What's the difference between Axelrod and Longdale? One street separates them but other than their names, they look exactly the same. So, in actuality, every day I drive through one very long town with twelve names.

When I walk into my office my Professional persona takes over completely, the memory of Hannah being inaccessible in that state of mind. As a Professional I am efficient, I make decisions quickly, and I watch the clock. I think, I plan, I do. I know where I am going and what it takes to get there. And the minute I am in my office and doing Professional, the rest of my life falls away. In sessions, I encourage clients not to cut themselves off from their wants and their feelings, yet my Professional does that splendidly.

My minimalist office decor reflects my Professional's preference for no frills, no fuss. I have three chairs, a floor lamp, a small table (to hold kleenex and appointment cards), and an oversized roll-top desk which I roll closed when clients come in. Everything I need and nothing I don't.

This Monday at the office, however, is not as streamlined as my Professional likes. Moving through the day is like traveling down an unpaved road in the dark. Impediments I don't expect trip me up and the path I think I know isn't clear. Long-standing clients cancel their appointments for later in the week. The light bulb in my lamp has burned out and the replacement in my desk is no good. A lady lost and looking for the restroom, wanders into a session by mistake, becomes very interested in what we are doing, and doesn't leave until I escort her out.

With all the no-shows and cancellations for the week, my lost income is several hundred dollars. On the drive home, I figure it out precisely — $360. I also recognize the pattern — when I count my income before I earn it, it usually doesn't materialize.

I hate days like this. The waiting and the worry wear me out faster than work does. That's another freedom of private practice — the freedom to worry all the time. It is after dark when I turn the key in my front door. I am exhausted. I leave my briefcase and my purse on the floor in the living room and kick off my shoes. I collapse in the blue chair, the one in which, just hours earlier, I had closed my eyes in anticipation of speaking with Hannah. Now I'm not thinking about her. I don't remember my commitment to her from last night. I am still halfway in my Professional persona. The other half of me is very tired and very, very frustrated.

I listen to other people all day long. Why is there never anyone to listen to me? Years ago, I decided that that wouldn't stop me from talking. With my eyes closed and my feet up I start speaking to the silence in my living room, lit only by the street lamp outside my window.

"Thank you for asking. I'm worn out. A lousy day. Not at all what it was supposed to be."

"Days like this are quite annoying." The thought is very close to mine.

"I can't afford this. And I want to work. I love my work. It's the nonsense — other people not following through with their commitments — that drains me."

"You shouldn't have to put up with that."

"Right," and a second later I bolt upright as I open my eyes. Someone else is speaking these words aloud! Sitting across from me in the dim room in the green upholstered chair with its mahogany-clawed feet is a woman. I can't see her clearly but I feel her presence in the room. She looks toward me and it makes me fidget.

"Do I know you?" I think I do but I don't remember an introduction.

"Yes, very well," and she opens her appointment book. I can tell it's an appointment book even in the shadows because it is just like mine with the flap that fastens on the right side. Now it lies open on her lap. "Yes, you know me very, very well indeed." She needs to say no more. I recognize that tone. It is mine when I am focused.

I can focus intently when I'm working on a project or toward a goal. I have no peripheral vision and I am never distracted. I forge ahead non-stop at whatever it is I am doing — painting my bedroom, writing reports, cleaning my condo — until both the job and I are finished.

And this is that focused, achieving part of me! This is my Controller sitting in my living room. I can't see her eyes clearly but I can tell that she wears glasses. Her feet rest on the floor and her head doesn't move.

This is the part of me that I had relied upon to get me through graduate school and to set up my business. Those were both huge goals that I achieved completely on my own. On my own except that it was she, this Controller, who took over and showed me how. Working that hard for that long doesn't happen without intense drive; she is my driver.

She has told me many times, "Your life is what you make it." "You only have yourself to rely on." "Don't waste time, do it now." She is the part of me who believes that she can create anything she wants and that whatever exists is to her credit. Not only is she a hard worker, she is a planner and an organizer. She will take control of this amorphous time — my life — and give it form. She will shape it exactly as she pleases. She has no doubts about her ability to do anything she wants. It just takes a decision and a willingness to work. Her decision, my work.

Sitting here with her in the semi-dark of my living room, I feel her iciness. Even when she isn't speaking I sense an inflexibility which tells me that there will be no discussion, no consideration of any alternatives. She is so completely sure within herself about what is right that she has no need to hear another viewpoint.

I can feel that one-pointed focus now, just sitting with her. And I realize that even though I hadn't recognized her, I have always felt her. This sternness which has been directed towards me has intimidated me for many years. Unquestioningly, I have obeyed the dictates which I felt in my bones. They were irresistibly compelling, as only unnamed forces can be.

Now, however, with my fatigue and my resignation, I just sit here. I don't speak. I feel her presence and I feel her disapproval. I couldn't have tolerated that earlier in my life but tonight after years of work and achievement and with my restlessness, I don't care. Whatever she thinks of me doesn't matter anymore.

With that recognition, I feel a chilling wave as her anger washes over me. I shiver and reach for the throw. When I turn back she is gone. Her coldness lingers, however. She hates me for ignoring her. I sit here in the dark and the cold and reflect upon how many years I have lived by her rules without ever hearing them distinctly, without knowing that I had a choice.

"I've wasted my life," I think. "I did everything my Controller told me to do for decades and here I am in the dark, feeling her disapproval. I have invested so much in my clients and nothing into my own life."

I can't live by her rules anymore although I don't know what living without her is like. I shout into the darkness, "What is going on? Have I entered the Twilight Zone? I have no idea what to do." And without warning, sobs burst from deep in my chest. Regret races through me.

Success has cost me so much. I've paid with my joy and my spontaneity. I seldom laugh. I never dance. I don't even know what I want. I am hurt and sad and bitterly disappointed. And I did this to myself. How could I be so wrong?

"I give up," I declare. "I cannot do anymore. I am defeated. I surrender."

"Well, finally," Hannah's voice crackles. "You do drag things out, sweetie. You know what I mean? I've been waiting for you but I couldn't get your attention." After turning on a lamp she stands by the fireplace leaning on the mantel, eating grapes from her pocket. Suction pulls the grapes through her pursed lips leading to a thwump. She wears a rose-colored sweatsuit with a roadrunner design on the front. The bird's legs are twirling in a blur while he goes nowhere. Her hair is the same frizzy mess as last night. One bobby pin dangles behind her right ear.

"Hannah! It has been an awful, awful day. My Controller was here; did you see her? She hates me. I'm confused — I don't know what I'm going to do, but I just can't keep doing what I've done all my life! I don't know what else there is, though."

I don't usually act desperate but tonight I do and I am way beyond caring how I appear. Especially to Hannah. She already knows me. Why pretend?

"I know you've been lost, dear," Hannah says with a grape on her cheek. "You haven't known what you were doing for quite a long time. You've been spinning your wheels. I'm glad you realize it now. We couldn't talk until you were ready."

"Did you hear me call to you this morning? I set aside 15 minutes for you."

"You can't schedule me! I won't fit into your neatly arranged little life." Hannah leans over the coffee table, picks up a magazine, Stress Reduction for Professionals, and lets out a snort as she throws it down. "I'm here to help you, honey. There's so much more going on than you know and when you realize that, well then . . ." and a coughing fit overtakes her until she spits a grape out onto the fireplace. Recovering, she looks around the room. I take her squint as a cue to turn on the other lamp.

"That's better," and she sits in the window seat with the street light coming from behind her. "Annie, you've got this whole thing all wrong. You run yourself ragged and think you're a success but you're not. Success isn't having money and worrying all the time. The 'good life' you say you want isn't built on anxiety and fear. You have done everything your Controller wanted. And look at you. You are a wreck. You may be respectable in your profession, but, honey, as a person, you're just not cutting it.

"You cling to your worry as though it were a diamond, too precious to release. You love your worry. You're lost without it.

"Why the hell would you rather be worried than have fun? That's crazy! You're crazy, girl. I think you're beginning to understand that, aren't you, sweetie?"

She smiles gently, as though she were a good friend kidding me when she acknowledges how mixed up I am. Too tired to be offended, I agree with her. She's right. Without realizing it, I had used my Controller to get a degree, a license, an office, a condo, and lots of toys. But now I want peace. I had thought that peace would come with success. But now I see that what it took to be successful — the Controller qualities of drive and self-denial – is not at all what it takes to be content. Success without peace inside is hollow.

"OK, Hannah, I'm ready for you. I know I can't do anything more on my own. I've used up all my tricks. I've gone as far as I can go with the Controller and I know she's disgusted with me. I can't live in her stranglehold any longer. Help me find another way."

"I've been waiting quite a while for you to ask. You certainly take your time." A devilish grin stretches across her face.

I have no idea what I am in for.

CHAPTER 3
LISTS

The rest of the week at the office isn't that different from Monday but my reaction to it is. I work fewer than half the hours I had scheduled due to cancellations and I use my "free" time (a strange phrase for lost income) to rest and daydream and make lists.

When I can't do anything else, I make lists. Lists comfort me. When I make a list, I feel like I have actually accomplished something, even though it's just in my mind. Having a list is almost as good as taking action. The only thing better is checking items off a list.

A list defines what it means to be alive today by naming activities that I think are useful to do. A list gives me guideposts — I'm halfway there or I can stop now that the list is completed. A list tells me what it takes to be a success. And a list confines my anxiety. When I wonder about being effective as a human, I list the specific jobs I want to finish today that would validate my worth. That limits my fear that I'm missing something.

I give my power to lists. "Am I OK?" translates to "Did I complete my to-do list?" A list is something specific to work with and, therefore, handleable.

Of course, the thing about lists is that they are usually short-term. They replace themselves daily. It's frustrating when tomorrow's list is similar to today's. That's my definition of depression: a to-do list that is the same for three days in a row.

This week when nothing much happens around me I occupy my mind with lists. Lists of questions to ask Hannah the next time she comes. On Tuesday my list looks like this:

—Do you know the Controller?

—How old is she? How old are you? Why do you women tell me different things? Who is right?

—Why do you smoke? Don't you know it's bad for you?

—Why were you dressed so neatly on Monday night? (I didn't mention my judgment of her previous appearance.)

—When did you start reading my thoughts? How long have you been part of me?

—Where were you when I was a kid? I know where the Controller was — right with me. Every move I made I heard her comments. But you, I couldn't even feel.

On Wednesday, my list is less self-centered:

—What do you do when we're not talking? (I am getting an inkling that maybe I am not the center of Hannah's life although it took me three days to even consider that possibility. And considering it, I still need to ask.)

—What do you do for fun? You tell me I'm no good at playing, so how's it done?

—You seem to like preparing food. Why? I never have found anything at all to appreciate about the time and effort it takes to cook. And there's nothing to show for it in the long run.

On Thursday I am feeling particularly shaky and my list reflects my insecurities:

—Where's the money? Do you care? Do you know? Most important, will you tell?

—How will I pay my bills if I listen to you and surrender? Isn't passivity dangerous?

—Are you leading me away from a respectable life as a professional into hippy-dippy spirituality? You know I'm not interested in that.

—Do you have any prescient notions about the stock market?
And on Friday:

—The workweek is over and I haven't done too much. What's

for the weekend? (Always when it's time to shift gears I encounter a different kind of anxiety. I know what I'm doing at work — until this week, that is — but at play, well, as Hannah says, I'm not too good at playing. I read that sentence after I wrote it and fear that I am imitating Hannah's speech patterns. More anxiety.)

—I know how to achieve, Hannah, but what do I do when I can't do anymore? What did you mean by "be and not do"? Have you seen the bumper sticker, "Don't just do something, sit there"? Sounds like your advice to me.

—When I'm not doing something, I feel guilty. I will give up doing things if you guarantee me I'll still be safe and if you take away the guilt. OK? (Another adopted Hannah-ism. She is influencing me.)

—If I trust you, what can I expect? Is this a paradox in which I release everything and then you yell "Surprise" and give it all back and more? Can I expect to gain from our deal?

The last question sounds embarrassingly self-serving and I know that isn't the attitude that fits here. But, hey, that's what I think. I can do this trust thing for a while and if it doesn't work out I can return to . . . what? My work is slowly falling away. I have a core group of clients, enough to pay the bills, but forget any vacation plans and skip the discretionary shopping. If this Hannah-proposed endeavor doesn't work out, I don't have a fallback position.

Realizing that my anxiety shoots through the top of my head and bounces off the ceiling, washing back down over me so that every fiber of my being reverberates with fear. I sit with my list on the desk in front of me and the pen is still in my right hand but I can't move. My breath is about 1/4 of an inch deep and my eyes won't focus. I don't hear anything except my heart beating — pounding — in my cavernous chest.

In this second I can't remember any helpful thoughts and certainly not any plans. I see very clearly and without doubt that I can't save myself. And with that awareness, my fear escalates to terror. Way down to the marrow of my bones.

I don't know what is happening in my body but I know I have felt this way before. And I don't want to feel it again. But what I want or don't want is irrelevant; the dreaded feelings have already overtaken me and I am pulled into a place I wish didn't exist. An all too familiar place I have visited before.

It's the place behind the burning, longing feeling that starts at the base of my throat and moves down into my chest. It plugs up my windpipe and makes it hard to breathe. The pressure tells me that something is not right, that something is missing, and that whatever that something is, it is important and without it, I'm not alive. Not really, truly living in the way that all of me feels alive.

Coming back to this place now, I see that I lost parts of myself some time ago. I lost my excitement and my joy and my laugh and my honest sadness. And without my own true feelings, without my insides, I want to weep.

That is when I know they're missing. Most times I'm so numb I don't even know what life could be. I don't see the colors because I've taught myself to think that the grays and the shadows are all that exist.

And I'm pretty good at moving through the shadows and I think I'm cool and I'm smart and that I have this trip down and that I'm on top of this thing I call my life. I've found my stride and I'm moving down the highway and nothing can stop me.

And then the tiniest crack, the smallest stone, trips me up. And I fall on my knees and I can't see the sky and I know, I know it where I know all things true, I know that this so-called life I've been living is a sham. A real shame because what I know then in that second is that, baby, I'm not alive at all. What I need to be alive, I lost a long, long time ago. That when I plugged up that ache that kept me weeping and stopped me from sleeping, then I lost my heart and, darn, if a piece of my soul wasn't attached. When I cut off my insides I could sleep, sort of, and do my business, and look like everyone else which was all I wanted. Then I didn't care about my poetry and my song and the flight of my heart. I just wanted to stop bawling. And, so, it was worth it.

And I did look like the rest of them. Sort of. And I quit crying when I saw babies and mothers and all the things I couldn't have.

And a drink now and again helped me through the night.

And the weeks passed and the years and that ache, well, it almost disappeared, but as the song says, "when the road is too lonely and the night gets too long," I feel my aloneness, that isolation that is so total that no one can possibly understand and I can't find words to describe it, that isolation that scares me so much that I think I won't ever come back from it, that I will be swallowed by the blackness and disappear and no one will even notice and, hell, no one will care.

No one knows who I am anyway. So, there is not another robot walking down the street in a navy blue business suit. So, what? So, what if my life ends? I ended it myself a long time ago when I closed off my heart when I gave away my soul. I didn't even sell myself for pieces of silver. A betrayal and for what? I betrayed my own self and not for anything. Not for money. Not for love. Not for prestige. Just to be invisible. So I wouldn't hurt any longer. Well, congratulations. I don't. Or do I?

Sitting here in my office I know I can't avoid myself. I'm faced with The Bottomless Pit and that's all I have. I'm in The Bottomless Pit and I'm falling and I can't see a way out. There isn't any light and there isn't anyone around. There's no help. And I feel like I will die here, falling through The Bottomless Pit and falling and falling. And I hope I do die because dying would be easier than feeling the despair of the isolation, that airless suffocating clammy heat. That loneliness that I have never bridged and don't believe that I ever can. Not really.

I've tried love. I thought that was what love was for, to stave off that blackness. I thought love was a drug that would numb me. I thought love could snag me out of The Bottomless Pit. Isn't love supposed to change reality, to illuminate the background magic, and bring it to the foreground? To let me be alive? I hoped love would erase my state of exile. I feel more alive when I'm part of someone else, but is it my life?

Really, I want to be connected to something deep in me, that something that I've lost, that something way inside my own heart, but I am afraid. And the love lets me think I can be whole again without going through all the ugly hurts.

But I get crazy needy when I'm in love. I always was crazy but I didn't know it. It's the need and the longing. Not that the hurt is dulled. It's always there. And the fear. I long for something to erase the fear.

I lose myself in a lover. That melting together isn't really a connection, though. It leads me away from myself. When I'm in love I feel less capable and less competent and more needy and more and more desperate and less connected to myself or to anyone else really. But any more I'm unable to tolerate that unanchored floating. Something real has to matter.

And the love ends. It always does and I'm left with the desperation and the desperation drives me further away from myself. I don't know if I'm going to survive. I'm not sure my will is strong enough and will is all, it seems like, that can drag me through.

I sit on the floor, these old mean feelings filling the office, and I sob. I'm in another time, a time I thought had passed. But my past found me. When I'm caught in these feelings it seems like I'm the only one awake in the whole world and my will is all I have and my will isn't strong enough. There's no hope, there's no one else I can touch, and my solitude is complete. I can't fight it anymore. I've got no more strength.

As I sit on my office floor with my feelings, night falls. I look into the night and it's thick. I surrender because I can't think of anything else to do. I can't cut my way through the blackness. It's too big and I don't have a direction to go, anyway, and, so, there really is nothing to do but sit.

And so what if the sobs come and so what if I think I'll die from the pain? It doesn't matter because it feels like I'm dead already. If I fall over and close my eyes it would have more integrity than walking around in this lie I call my life. And I announce my defeat: LIFE, YOU WIN.

There's no point trying to hide it. Once I know it myself, once I know this game of fitting in with everyone else won't work, I can't keep playing it. So, I sit in the dark and I sob. I've got nothing but my hurt. I'm already defeated, and I've got no hope.

I don't know how long I sit on the floor of my office and sob into my crossed arms before I sleep. I awake with the moonlight beating on my eyelids. My first thought is of my last client, the one I was waiting for when my reverie kidnapped me. She must not have shown. I am thankful for that. For the first time in my career, I appreciate a no-show. I pull myself up and drive home in the early morning hours.

Those old feelings have been with me forever. I could not articulate them for many years but the emptiness and the fear were the same feelings I had felt in childhood without having defining labels. Tonight I let them all come — the loneliness and the fear and the hurt and the desperation. Those feelings have terrified me most of my life and I have fought them — most effectively with my mind. But tonight I don't fight; I surrender.

I drive the coast route home while the moonlight dances on the breaking waves. And I feel freer than I have felt in a very, very long time.

CHAPTER 4
A GRAY SKY

Saturday is one of the handful of drizzly overcast days that settle on southern California each year. The gorgeous sunny not-too-hot weather can get tiresome and I always enjoy the break a gray sky provides. This Saturday I enjoy it in a deep sleep. I arise early in the afternoon, embracing my pillow and dreaming of flying with a man I haven't yet met.

I stumble from my bedroom to the kitchen, make a cup of peppermint tea, and slouch in the blue chair. I look out the front window, open an inch. The smell of the damp air reminds me of my grandmother's linen closet — sweet and fresh, tinged with lilacs. The humidity plumps the air into a comforter. A weak light sneaks through the clouds and haunts the trees and the sidewalk and the street, framed by my window. An infrequent car races through the surreal setting and disappears into what must have been a normal reality, existing just outside my field of vision.

Even with the cool breeze from the window, I am warm in my old white chenille robe and oversized pink formerly fuzzy slippers. After two years and a few washings, the slippers are stringy and matted. My big toes peek through small holes. The soles have long ago molded to my feet and carry the impression of the balls of my feet and my toes even when my feet aren't in them. I pull my legs up underneath me and balance the teacup on my knee.

I feel just like the day looks — a bit otherworldly. I sip the steaming tea. The cup warms my hands and the sweet scent fills the empty spaces in my head. Today I have nowhere to go and time doesn't matter. I am just here.

What an incredible experience yesterday evening was. For a few hours, a slice of my life was cut out, and another reality — or unreality — was inserted. Only once before had I felt like I was walking without gravity in a world with different natural laws. During my sophomore year in college, my roommate and I went to her boyfriend's room during a party in football season. We smoked his Acapulco Gold and drank tequila with him. Clouds of hazy smoke had filled his dark, closed room. We lay sideways across the two twin beds pushed together, dangling our feet over the edge, each of us caught in our private hallucinations.

I watched as monsters emerged from the corners of the ceiling and pounced on me. Without words they let me know that they hated me and were committed to killing me. They despised my cowardice. I was not fit to walk on the planet. If I would not pick up the knife and plunge it into my heart they would make my life miserable.

I didn't and they did. I have not let myself be out of control since then. I have lived as a hostage to the threats of these unseen demons. Unseen but very, very real. Last night was the second time I have experienced the intense power which comes from inside me but which doesn't feel like the me I know.

My hand shakes as the memory of that college afternoon fills my body and I spill tea on the carpet. I go to the kitchen for a towel to blot it and find my Controller waiting for me. She leans against the oven with her arms crossed. I reach around her for the black and white towel hanging on the oven door. She warns, "If you listen to me, we can fight them. I'm your only hope."

A shiver races up my spine as I turn away from her and take the towel back to my chair. "That woman frosts my bones," I think. I pull my robe around my neck and hold it closed with my left hand as I sit down and pat the wet carpet with the towel in my right.

All of a sudden I'm not comfortable. Having the whole afternoon to myself becomes not a luxury but a burden. My anxiety returns. My mind shifts to fourth gear and I stand up. Only when I am upright do I realize that I have nowhere to go. I sit down again, neither the tea nor the day being of interest to me now.

"No, I'm not going to do this. I don't need to be nuts. Today is for me," I tell myself. And I close my eyes. I want to be back in the sleep world with my flying partner. Things made as much sense there as they do here and there was a lot more fun.

I close my eyes and look for Alex. I have always liked that name and so I give it to my flying companion from a few hours ago. I see myself swim through cotton ball clouds calling his name.

My arms strain from the effort and I am ready to give up. The clouds open to a meadow with yellow and white poppies dotting low blue-green grass. Alex is on the other side of the field and he is laughing. He opens his arms to me, inviting me to come.

My heart wants to join him but I can't lift my feet. I try to call out, to tell him I am coming, not to go, to please, please, wait for me but I can't find my voice. My legs become concrete; no matter how hard I try, I can't lift them. Alex grows fainter and fainter and then he evaporates.

As I sit in the blue chair with my eyes closed, a tear runs down my cheek.

CHAPTER 5
REALITY

After my experiences this week, real and not real become artificial distinctions, simply unspoken agreements that make conversation possible. I realize that to me whether something is physically real or not real does not define its importance. Is Hannah less real than the mess in my bedroom? To me, she is more real. Certainly, she is more important. The mess I can clean up and it will be gone but her effect on me lingers when she's not around.

Alex is another case. I glimpsed him but I hadn't connected. Can I trust that he is real? I don't have a strong sense of him but somehow, I know that I will see him again.

My Controller is more real to me than most people I have met. The tone of her anger and the strictness of her rules have influenced me more than anything I have been told by anyone. Now she seems to be fading. Her voice is still firm but harder to hear. I sense a distance from her. Now I have a choice. I can listen to her or not. So, my Controller is real but my relationship with her is changing.

Then, who am I? I cringe when I ask myself that question. Not another boomer with a melodramatic mid-life identity crisis. I don't want to be reducible to a sappy song played on the radio asking if this is all there is or insisting on doing life my way. I don't know what is happening in me but I know it is worth taking seriously, or no, it is worth not being overly serious. I mean, I take it as significant but I have to keep my perspective and my sense of humor. Important things I can't be too somber about.

Is Hannah taking over my brain?

These changes I notice happening in me are a surprise. But as I let go of my absolute need to know what is going on, of my expectations about what might occur in the future, of my formerly rational thinking process, and of my sanity, I can relax and enjoy the ride. I feel like I am on a train operated by something or someone I don't know, going somewhere I can't predict, at a very rapid pace. The good part is that as long as I don't become overly intellectual, I can imagine that I am in a plush deep red private compartment and that I am safe. Not thinking is crucial to maintaining this orientation. As soon as my mind gets involved, I am lost.

So, to stay away from thinking, I take a drawing class. I learn "to see." Seeing what is around me has never been a priority; I have always been so preoccupied with my feelings and my thoughts that I haven't paid much attention to the outer world.

From this class, I learned to notice details that aren't personally significant — the subtle variations in the color of green in the leaves of a ficus tree, the grass, and my rose bush. I see how the blue of the sky doesn't melt into the blue of the ocean but meets it in a sliver of a horizon that is a different shade from either the sky blue or the ocean blue. I see the flatness of the landscape at dusk when the light is horizontal and buildings at short range lose their depth. Meeting my inner world figures has given me a different slant on reality; now I see my outer world with a new vision, too.

Seeing doesn't happen when I look. Seeing requires a un-focus that allows me to receive. This is a shift. My mind likes to be sharp and my faith has always aligned with my ability to bore through any problem with pointed logic and reach a solution. My art teacher, Rita, lets me know that this is exactly the wrong approach if I want to see.

"Seeing is being the object. Imagine that you are inside what you are looking at. You can look back and see yourself looking.

But when you really really see," (and here she rolls her "r's" so that her "reallys" strain to escape her throat) "then you become one with the object. You no longer look at it. You see the way it sees."

When she says that I am ready to walk out of class but that would have been awkward with the bodies sprawling on the floor and the drawing pads leaning every which way against chairs and easels and desks. And more than anything I want to be appropriate. So, I pretend to pay attention.

"Now, children," she continues, talking to this group who are mostly over 60, "I want you to draw what you see when you see this bowl of apples. Don't look at it. SEE IT!"

I look at it. And I keep looking at it. And I think, "This is why California has a reputation for being flaky." But I am trapped for another two hours. I hope we won't spend the whole time SEEING.

Other people seem to be getting glimpses of some ineffable verity but I just stare at the bowl of apples, elevated on a stool on top of the desk in the middle of the room. Red apples in a low white bowl about eight inches in diameter.

Is this what Cezanne did? I love his paintings of apples. I can feel them just by looking at them. Thinking of Cezanne's apples, I look at the ones in front of me dreamily. Maybe he looked at apples just like these.

When I look at his apples, I always imagine they are inviting me to taste them. And I want to, standing in front of his paintings, seeing the drops of water on their peels, the ripe fullness of their fruit. I even believe they are chilled and crispy. My mouth waters.

And in that second, I SEE. I know what it is like to be an apple from the inside, not from the outside as something to look at but as a living and, yes, even a breathing entity. My excitement runs through my arm into my hand and I draw the most luscious, sensuous apple that has ever been drawn in an Adult Ed art class. I'm not simply copying the lines my physical eyes scan. I am living inside the apple and being the apple. I'm not on time and I'm not doing the class assignment. I am experiencing apple-ness.

The bell rings in what seems like seconds and I look at the clock which has mysteriously jumped ahead two hours. I have SEEN. I gather my equipment and stumble out the door. I walk home in a trance, still not believing what I have just experienced.

So, this is what Rita means.

For the next weeks, I practiced SEEING. (I will always hear that word in capital letters because of Rita's emphasis.) I sit in the park and I SEE the newly planted sapling, the wet dirt at its base having been hollowed into a bowl that rises two inches at the rim. Its slender trunk sprouts four branches, none with a leaf yet. The spring breeze is cold and strong but the young tree resists its pull.

As my gaze softens, I imagine that I am inside the tree. From the outside, I would have guessed that the tree is struggling and unrooted. (Since that's what I feel, it is easy to imagine the tree in that same state.) When my imagination moves inside the tree, I feel strength. The new plant has already sent stabilizing roots into the soil. I can imagine that it says, "Here I am, world. I'm going to show you a tough, proud, tall tree. Watch me grow."

I smile as I sense that confidence and enthusiasm. This is fun.

I practice SEEING people, too. I watch an older woman bundled up on the bench across from the slide and imagine, from my point of view, what it is like to be her. I guess that she may be lonely with no place else to go and that she does not really want to be here.

Then I un-focus my gaze and move my imagination inside her body and listen. What I receive is different from what I assumed. I "hear" from inside her that she is considering a huge decision, one that will change her life forever, and that she is confused. She has come to the park to let her thoughts roam.

It doesn't take long for me to notice the difference between what I first think from my perspective as an observer and what I receive as the other person's truth when I move my intuition inside her. I need to know that I can trust what my imagination/intuition tells me.

My mind suggests an experiment. Check out my intuitions. Ask if what I receive is really what the other person feels. The non-verbal objects of my attention are left out of this trial as are strangers whom I would never approach suggesting that I had read their thoughts. (No matter how wacky my ideas get, I always conduct myself respectably.) Fortunately, I am still doing a few hours of therapy each week and there I find the subjects for my experiment.

The identified problems that clients present in therapy are never the ones that we need to work with. They are merely symptoms of some underlying block. If a woman hasn't grieved a loss from decades ago, she won't be able to appreciate people and relationships currently. She may present the problem that her husband is inattentive and preoccupied with his job, not noticing how his distraction serves her need to keep distance in their relationship. She benefits from the distance which she uses as a shield against her vulnerability. Her pain, still unhealed from childhood, remains locked inside her.

Lydia is such a client with just that profile. She is not psychologically-oriented, a phrase that describes a person's ability to think in terms of needs and motivations. Nor is Lydia particularly self-aware. She is angry. She knows what she wants but she doesn't know how to make it happen and that is why she is consulting me. In her mind, she figures that three, maybe four, sessions should be sufficient for me to tell her how to change her husband into Mr. Consideration and give her the marriage she says she wants.

It's a truism that if we want to know what we really choose and not what we say we choose, we should look around us. What exists is what we (unconsciously) choose. I used to say that to clients but their howls of protest suggested that they didn't trust that I was on their side. With Lydia, I attempt subtly to encourage her to take responsibility for the facts as they are. She prefers victimhood. At the top of her lungs.

Our next session is strained. Lydia is annoyed that she isn't getting the results she wants and lets me know that she has wasted her money coming to see me. She sits across from me in a full-skirted yellow dress with multi-colored pumps. Her hat occupies the third chair and her purse rests on the floor. Her anger pulls her eyebrows together and narrows her eyes. Her lips purse the way a seam in a dress does when you pull the basting thread. I feel her venom. It reminds me of my Controller and I suppress a shiver.

As her eyes glare at me and her mouth scolds me I soften my gaze and watch her face become hazy. Her words punch towards me but they fall short of contacting me. I put myself inside her body. It feels strangulating-tense in there, utterly cold, and, beneath everything, terrified. Terrified in the way a baby who can't ensure her own survival must feel terrified. The kind of terror that reduces you to a simpering blob. I know that terror.

I focus on Lydia in that unfocused way, just feeling what it is like to be her on the inside. I move deeper within her. There really is a gentleness to her, beneath her insults, way way down inside her. Feeling that soft part of her, I am touched by the genuine caring that lives beneath her fear. I smile as I smiled at the tree. When I reach the core, whether of a tree or a person, I smile. We all share an experience of living.

Apparently, for several minutes Lydia has been hurtling accusations my way. I haven't been listening to her words; I am simply appreciating what a beautiful woman she is underneath all the camouflage.

Then I notice that she is silent.

"I'm sorry," I say, jerking back to attention. "I am seeing you in a totally different way from how I had seen you before and I am caught by your beauty and your sensitivity. I am taken with your softness. You really are a very very gentle person."

For the first time, Lydia doesn't have a word to share. Very slowly tears roll from the inside corners of her eyes while we keep perfect eye contact. The tears come faster and harder. I pull my chair next to hers as she bends over her lap, convulsed with the sobs that have been stuffed away for so long.

She cries magnificently. I am so grateful to share these exquisitely human moments with clients. Her tears provide the confirmation that my mind requires to test my intuition.

Driving home that evening I speak to Hannah. "When I can touch clients that way, Hannah, I feel excited. What more is there to life than being with someone who is opening up what has been forbidden territory and reclaiming her aliveness?" I feel very satisfied and don't expect an answer to my question. But, characteristically, Hannah does have a response.

"Opening up yourself, honey. Life isn't just for others. You have a right to your closed-off spaces, too. You have so much practice now going through it with clients, don't you think you're ready to jump into your own life?"

My throat tightens, my breathing becomes shallow, and I swerve over the dividing line into the next lane. The other driver's frantic honking expresses my reaction to Hannah's suggestion precisely.

CHAPTER 6
PEANUT BUTTER

Why do Hannah's words scare me? I sit with my tea and toast sans peanut butter the next morning watching the early morning light creep over the eastern horizon. The newspaper lies on the table, still rolled, with the unopened mail from yesterday. I have been working on a drawing of the tree. My drawing pad leans against the fireplace, positioned so that I can look at it from anywhere in my living/dining room. I enjoy that little tree but I haven't captured its determination on my paper.

This Saturday morning, I am irritable. My neck is stiff on the left side so I can't turn my head to the right easily. Is this what getting old feels like? I'm not ready to be old.

I look at my last tea bag slumped in the saucer and remind myself to buy more tea and some groceries, too. My signal to buy groceries is seeing the bottom of the peanut butter jar. Today not only have I seen it, there is no peanut butter at all left. I always put off shopping until the last of the peanut butter is gone and today is that day. I decide to go to the store now, early, before shoppers crowd it. Without make-up and in my most comfortable baggy cords and gray sweatshirt, I drive four minutes to the new Shop and Save. I did shop but I doubt that I saved. Not that I'm an impulse buyer. On the contrary, I don't buy what I need because I either don't want to spend the money, I don't know how to prepare it, or I just don't care.

I have survived on peanut butter and jelly for months at a time and I still love it. When I'm celebrating, I eat peanut butter and apple sandwiches. When I run out of bread and jelly, I have peanut butter on an iced tea spoon dipped in honey. Peanut butter goes with graham crackers, granola, and waffles. I've even read some cookbooks that use it in a sauce over rice. One of my favorite treats is peanut butter with frozen bananas in a smoothie. Peanut butter has saved me from starvation many times.

I make a beeline for the peanut butter shelf, passing the fresh produce that the box boy unloads. I think eating fresh fruit and vegetables is a very good idea and I plan to start doing so soon, maybe very soon. But for now, I know I can count on peanut butter, crunchy and salted, and I know where to find it.

I turn the corner into the peanut butter aisle and I see Alex at the other end. At first, I recognize him as someone familiar but not someone I can place. When it dawns on me who he is, he has disappeared. I forget my basket and dart to the spot where he stood. In the process, I knock over a stack of instant oatmeal boxes waiting to be shelved. When I reach the end of the aisle he is gone. I look down both adjacent aisles but glimpse no one.

"In a hurry, lady?" the postpubescent box boy asks. A mustache sprouts on his upper lip. I've seen Pete in here before and he's always ready to chat.

"I thought I saw a friend but he must have left."

"No one here this early but you," Pete responds. I walk slowly back to the peanut butter section, suddenly uncomfortable that I've not showered and dressed for the day. I want to pay for my goods and leave.

After I put away my few purchases I again sit at my table, this time with a cup of hot water since I forgot to buy tea. I speak to Hannah. I find it comforting to have someone who is always listening. So, although I don't see her, I address my comments to her.

"Hannah, my life is getting increasingly bizarre and I want some straight talk from you. What is going on? Why do I see Alex but never meet him? Why is my Controller angry? What is happening to me? If you would just give me a clue, I could get on with it, whatever <u>it</u> is. I hate this confusion. This is so inefficient. Just tell me what you want me to do and let me do it."

Silence.

I had been clear. If she isn't responding, I'll wait. I feel tense. Something's wrong but I don't know what. I feel like a drive belt whose cogs are not meshing.

I'm reading Barbara Kingsolver's latest so I grab it and recline in the window seat. It doesn't take long to lose myself in Barbara's landscapes and not much longer to drift into sleep.

As with my morning, my sleep is disjointed and unsatisfying. I dream of struggling to climb over a rocky wall, cutting my hands and legs in the process. I am scared and confused. There is an urgency about getting to the other side and my time is running out. My breathing comes fast and I jerk myself awake, panting. Disoriented, I look around before putting my head back down.

Another two minutes and I'm again in dreamland but on a different continent. The meadow appears but Alex is not at the other side. I wade through the grass and the wildflowers, all the time calling his name. At the other side where I saw him last, I stepped into a hole and I fell and I kept falling. I can't catch myself and my panic awakens me.

Even sleep offers me no escape from my misery. I give up and slump into the blue chair. "Hannah!" I wail. "Please come to me now."

"All right, already. Sheesh. Such a whiner you are today. Woke up on the wrong side of the bed?" Hannah wears a red and white horizontal striped top and canvas pants.

"Yeah and on the wrong side of my life, too. I HATE THIS. I hate not being able to go through my days smoothly. I hate the fear and the fighting. I thought I was beyond that. I thought I was doing OK but my old anxiety is back today. I am so frustrated. I don't want to live this way anymore."

"And you've been doing so well," she muses, eyeing my drawing. "I thought you were having a good time." She walks across the room scrutinizing the tree.

"Yes, well, I was. Until last night. What did you do to me? Ever since my drive home, I have been out of sorts and unhappy."

"Out of sorts, I'll say. Downright mean. You know you're not much fun when you pout."

Suddenly, I understand. I <u>had</u> been having fun. Until I asked

Hannah for clarification in the car last night. I recognize the moment when my "mood" had changed. And now I get that she truly had done it. Realizing that she is the culprit, I vehemently repeat my question.

"What the hell did you set off in my brain? I was doing fine and then you came into my head and messed up the works. What are you doing?"

"My, my, my, my, my. We are feeling particularly sorry for ourselves this morning." She stands up straight and her tone changes. "Snap out of it. You don't have time to mope around. You have to be ready."

I look at her as she makes this Controller-type pronouncement. "Well, get with it!" She waits for me to do something but, as usual, I don't know what that is. "Move it!" Hannah bellows and points to the bathroom.

"You want me to get cleaned up?" Even to myself, I sound like a dopey ten-year-old. Hannah keeps her arm straight and her index finger pointed. No one has ever spoken to me this way.

However, I am glad to have some concrete, clear action to take. I emerge dressed and made up forty minutes later and expect to find her in my living room. Not only is Hannah there, my Controller is in the green chair, and two other women I haven't seen before are sitting in the window seat. One is leafing through my book and the other is looking at the bicycle race passing by outside in the street.

I don't know what to say and I don't feel like the hostess as much as a defendant in a trial. Thankfully, Hannah speaks.

"That's better, Anne. Now we're all here because you're ready for the next step." I start to ask what's the next step, but Hannah raises her voice as she raises her hand and speaks quickly.

"You can't live the way you've been living any longer. You said so yourself this morning and we're here to support you in moving on."

So, these are friends?

"Friends, yes, sort of, but not exactly." This is the Hannah I know. What comes next, I wonder warily.

"Quiet," she cautions me, trespassing on my thoughts. "You've met Helen, already," and she indicates the Controller. This is the first time I really look at her in full daylight. Helen isn't nearly as intimidating in the light as she is in the dark or in my mind.

She looks old and a bit sad. Her mouth droops on one side as though she has lost control of those muscles and can no longer keep her lips even. She wears a dark print dress with a small belt and walking shoes. She seems tired. The words "worn out, deflated and used up" skip through my head. She meets my gaze for a second before she looks away.

Hannah continues speaking. "And this is Marguerite." The young woman on my right sitting in the window seat smiles at me. She appears to be about 30 with finely detailed make-up. She moves her body gently and fluidly. I like her immediately.

She says with a slight accent. "Call me Maggie. I am so pleased that we have met. I love the work you are doing with your art but you need a few pointers." And Hannah cuts her off. "Thanks, Marguerite, but you two can talk later. And this is Theresa."

The woman who has been looking out the window turns back for just a moment. Is she bored? She doesn't seem interested in participating in the group which has assembled in my living room. Her dark hair is clasped at her neck and slithers down her back. Her crossed arms hide her hands. While not offensive, her appearance is not inviting.

"We are here at your request, Anne." I notice that Hannah hasn't used the diminutive Annie as she did when she was comforting me. I suspect that this is a business meeting.

"You have said it and we all heard it. You can't live this way any longer. Well, because you asked, we are here to help you."

And everyone looks at me. Suddenly, I feel self-conscious and unable to hide. No pretending with these folks.

Helen stands and announces as she walks toward the kitchen, "My job is done. I'm resigning as of today. When you were young you asked me to keep you alive and safe. I have done that for several decades now. Anne, you have learned what I have to give you. Use it well. But you don't need me around anymore." And she walks into the kitchen wall and disappears.

The room seems to lift a quarter of an inch. Hannah then addresses Theresa. "Will you please tell Anne who you are and why she needs to listen to you now?"

With what seems like a huge effort Theresa turns and faces the room and walks to the far side of the green chair. "My job is to teach you passion." I can't believe what I hear.

"Passion?" I ask. Theresa seems like the human definition of indifference.

Hannah intervenes. "You see what you've done with your passion? Theresa could be any way you allowed her to grow and develop and this is what you've chosen."

Why do I feel ashamed? "No, I . . ." and, as usual, Hannah asserts herself.

"Yes. Yes, Anne, look at her. Theresa is your creation."

Theresa sits on the floor hugging her knees but she looks at Hannah. For the first time, I notice dampness in her eyes. "Theresa wasn't even walking until you started drawing," Hannah offers.

I feel like I have been caught in a sneaky undercover caper and am now being exposed. Defensively, I reply that I don't know what she is talking about, but Hannah motions me over to Theresa. I sit on the floor next to her.

"OK, go on." Hannah is impatient. I know what she wants. I put my arm around Theresa's bony shoulders. Theresa is uncomfortable with that and so am I. But Hannah nods. Theresa and I sit there for several minutes. Her body softens as I hold her.

I practice seeing. Seeing isn't really the right word in this situation. It is more receiving and allowing myself to know. As I hold Theresa, I receive a visual impression of a malnourished toddler like the ones in the magazines who can be rescued for a dollar a month. I stay with that impression. My eyes close and I watch that toddler. She makes no sound but I can feel the wails lodged in her chest.

I hold Theresa tighter as I watch the toddler and I feel her body shake in my arms. The shakier she becomes the tighter I hold her. And, in the same way I do, she bursts into heart-wrenching sobs. She shrieks and moans. The disinterested young woman from the window seat hides inside her a passionate soul.

I hold her as she sways with grief and I grieve with her. It wasn't that different from what I had felt that night weeks ago on my office floor. Beneath the anxiety that revisited me last night and this morning lies an un-nurtured soul.

I know in my bones that it was my choice. I had turned my own child out, refusing to even recognize her. I had chosen to ignore my passion. I had disowned Theresa. I am guilty.

I don't know what Hannah and Marguerite are doing; I am only paying attention to Theresa. All of a sudden her tears and her cries cease and there is silence in the room broken only by the birds making getting-on-with-the-day noises. Theresa looks up at me, shyly at first. Then she kisses me lightly on the cheek and giggles.

"Thank you for being here," she whispers. Slowly, a smile spreads over her face. Her sadness lifts. Her body feels different under my arm, sturdier and vibrant.

"Let's have some fun!" Theresa exclaims.

Hannah, Marguerite, and I exhale our collective breath, sweeping the room clean of any leftover melancholy and, in relief, we giggle, too. Our mirth grows into a roar and we cling to each other, laughing so hard we topple over.

Whether they are thinking it also, I know they can hear my thoughts. I feel like our family is finally reunited. Together we are home.

CHAPTER 7
FEAR AND THE TREE

4:17 a.m. is too early for anyone to get up, especially for me. So, when I awake at that time the next morning I roll myself up tightly in my covers, mummy style, and I think. I think about my first encounter with Hannah and my reaction to her. She seemed so sloppy and I was critical of her. And I think about our subsequent contacts.

We were adversaries, each taking the measure of the other as we circled cautiously. The more critical my thoughts were of her, the more unappealing she looked to me. The better I grew to know her, the more I softened my gaze and the more I appreciated her. Interesting.

My thoughts influence how open my heart is. And her appearance reflects my heart. When my heart is gentle, Hannah is an attractive figure. <u>What</u> I see reflects <u>how</u> I see. Very interesting. My openness is key.

And now there are Theresa and Maggie. It is clear to me that they are parts of me whom I need to know but I am glad I'm not defending that position at a meeting of my colleagues. This strange world of fantasy people seems eerily familiar. I know the feelings these folks carry. I have always felt them. These individuals who have lived in me forever now insist that I acknowledge them, respect them and support them.

I am wending my way through this complex jungle of tangled feelings and camouflaged holes. The laws of this world are as sure as physical laws and just as irrefutable. What's unseen is real. Feelings are facts. What is, regardless of my mind's preference. In my head, I had known these truths from my training and my work with clients but now I am living them from my heart. I think about

Theresa. When I held Theresa while she cried, I thought about the evening in my office when I cried. And I thought about Lydia's crying with me. Without understanding what I was doing, I had moved one step at a time in healing that empty, hateful hole that has always burned in me. First, I felt my sadness. Then I supported Lydia in feeling hers. And then I had identified the part of me who is anguished, Theresa. It isn't all of me and that is reassuring to know.

As I snuggle in my bed I smile. The air in my room is cool but in my bed I am toasty. The early morning sun creeps between the slats in my vertical blinds casting yellow lines across the light gray carpet. One pillow reclines on the floor while the other is smashed nearly flat beneath my head. I feel soft in my covers, in the light, and inside me, as I lie in bed.

When I do emerge from my bedroom I find Hannah, Theresa, and Maggie sitting at the table. "Good morning," I say, as though nothing is unusual about having three people in my home at this hour. As soon as I speak they disappear.

What is this about? I ask myself. Their air lingers as I meander through my morning.

Calling in for my messages I learned that my one afternoon client had canceled so I packed a bag with three apples, a jar of peanut butter, and an iced tea spoon and I headed to the park to draw in the early morning light. Walking there I talk with Maggie whom I can feel with me but I can't see.

"I haven't been able to capture the spirit of the tree, Maggie, and I don't know why. I understand about moving inside the tree and I think I have, but I still can't convey its life."

And I hear her response inside my head as surely as if someone had spoken the words aloud. "You have to put yourself in your drawing. Don't be a camera. Let us feel your feelings when you see that tree. If you want to draw its spirit, you have to let it into your heart and then draw how that feels."

I sit on the bench facing the tree with the sun rising behind my head. The bench is wet with dew but it is woven metal and I can wipe the dew away easily. The air tweaks my nose while the early sun caresses my back. The light is new, washing the little park landscape in shades of yellow-white that make the wet grass and bushes look young.

Maggie's words intrigue me. Feel the spirit of the tree, let it into my heart, and then draw my feelings. This is getting weirder and weirder but why complain now? Thus far there has been a gift at every step of this strange journey so I am encouraged to trust that each new step is worth taking.

Maggie, now in physical form, sits next to me on the bench and directs my vision. "Do you notice the curve in the tallest branch? It grows out of the trunk at a 45-degree angle and then zooms up to the sky. What does that make you think of?"

I don't know. It's a branch, it has a pleasant shape, I like looking at it. But it is just a tree.

Reading my mind Maggie responds. "No, you need to see more than the outline of the tree. What do you feel when you look at the curve of that branch?"

This requires concentration. I have always resisted taking time. I like to work fast and to be finished. I don't like to dawdle.

"This isn't wasting time," Maggie interrupts impatiently. "You say you want to draw. You also say you're not getting the spirit of the tree on your paper. And I happen to know that you're not too satisfied in some other parts of your life, too."

I look at her accusingly. Was she referring to Alex or, more precisely, to his absence? Or even more globally, the absence of any men in my life? I feel defensive.

"So, drawing this tree will help me in the intimacy department?" I scoff. I can appreciate non-linear thinking. To a point. This is a leap.

"That's your way of saying it, but, yes." She is sweet and feminine. I am annoyed. How did I get cast as the ungainly resistant awkward one again? I want to be in her seat.

"That's what she's trying to show you, dear," and Hannah appears on my left. "Why don't you stop sparring with her and listen?" And, sarcastically, she adds, "You might learn something." I turn to respond to her sarcasm but she is gone. So,

I listen to Maggie and look at the tree. Maggie speaks while she looks at the tree, also.

"Notice the way each branch curves in a different direction yet they all seem to move together? When you look at the tree it looks like one piece, all the parts contribute, but when you look at each part, it seems distinctly individual."

Yeah, so what? I think, and I swear I am jabbed in my left ribs by an elbow that fits Hannah's arm.

"I see what you mean, Mags," I say sweetly or as close as I come to sweet. Fortunately, she's not as sensitive to my insincerity as Hannah is.

"Annie, what do you feel when you see the movement of the four branches, each reaching in a different direction?"

OK, concentrate, I tell myself. The slight breeze sways the branches. It is a peaceful scene. I enjoy looking at it, but . . . I feel nothing. I turn to Maggie and she is sitting on the back of the bench with her head resting on her fists, elbows on her knees. Without my saying anything, she speaks.

"I sit here and I'm glad to be here. This moment is so fine. Just being with you and with this tree, I feel like I'm sharing a moment of great vitality." And she puts her arm around my shoulder and squeezes without taking her eyes off the tree. She is too near the fringe for me to be comfortable. The rib jab is harder this time and I wince.

"Don't you feel it? Our being together? Our being immersed in this second together?" And she looks at the tree.

"Yeah, this is great, Mags," and I cover my left side. But Hannah is ready with a hard thump to the back of my head.

"Will you quit it, Anne?" Hannah whispers as loud as one can whisper and still have it qualify as a whisper. "Marguerite is generously, lovingly here AT YOUR REQUEST to be of service to you. And you're being a jerk. Would you like to participate in your life this morning? Or do you want to continue alone, always alone? It's up to you. MAKE UP YOUR MIND."

Maggie is still looking at the tree in rapture. I am embarrassed. I decide to look, too. Actually, I would be glad to be as happy as Maggie appears. I scoff but I know it's out of fear that I can't really have that happiness. And it's also out of hurt. Afraid to care again and to be disappointed again. So, I'm aloof and sarcastic and, yes, I'm a jerk. Hannah is right.

I sit quietly with Maggie. She seems excited. And I wonder what it is like to be that excited about sitting in the park so early in the day looking at a tree. So, I practice my SEEING with Maggie and I move my intuition inside her body. There is clarity and a joy in her that I seldom feel. She is excited about just being. For her, just to breathe is fun. And she truly means it when she talks about sharing this moment. She has a connection because she opens her heart and receives it. It isn't about extending, reaching out, or attempting. Maggie connects to me, to the day, to the tree, because her heart is open.

When I am there inside her body, I notice that any disconnection I feel is from blocks I put up, not from obstacles around me. There is nothing out there. There are no problems. There are no enemies. Only what my fear creates.

Seeing through Maggie's eyes is different from seeing through my own. Her seeing seems to come up from the ground, through her legs into her heart. Her heart opens. She isn't a doer, she is an acceptor. A receiver. She doesn't mold anything; she just receives.

What I feel when I sit there next to Maggie is what it is like to live with an open heart. And I learned that openness to myself, to my feelings, not to someone else.

I move my SEEING back inside me as if I were looking at another person and I see walls to block my feelings from myself. I see how I am afraid of me! I am afraid of my depth, my complexity, and my own intensity. I am afraid of losing myself in the rushing torrent of my emotions.

There isn't anyone else or anything else who is a threat to me. I'm not defending myself against anything outside me. I am trying to hold myself together rigidly, fearing the natural flow of my own feelings.

I SEE that I had forged a facade in iron approximately as flexible as the bench I am sitting on and that now it is time to walk away from it. That much rigidity only comes from fear. And I sit here and feel the fear that lives so deeply in me. I SEE it as though I were seeing it in another person and I sit with it and I feel it.

It is strange, allowing all this fear to run through my body while I sit on the bench not revealing anything. Maggie sits next to me and I can feel Hannah close, too. But nothing shows on my face or in my body. I am a container for this intense fear and I let it travel through me. Maggie looks at the tree and while I feel comforted that she sits next to me, there is no interaction between us. She dwells in her ecstatic world and I in my intense world. But, as she has said, there is a sense of togetherness.

We sit here for an hour. The fear is overwhelming and yet, because I can SEE, I watch it and I let it move. I count my breaths when the fear is particularly intense and I thank the bench for its support when I feel weak. And I just sit here.

Maggie doesn't speak to me but I can feel her breathing, too, and sometimes when the fear threatens to choke me, I align my breath with hers. We are breathed by the same air. That is reassuring because it tells me that no matter how upsetting or painful my feelings are, my fear is not bigger than life. My fear is here now but I am participating in life through my breath. The fear isn't ongoing or significant. But my breath is and the breath that breathes me is.

Maggie and I breathe and sit and look at the tree and I feel my fear. I don't own the fear; I just let it move through me. It has been wound up tight, like the inside of a golf ball, and when it comes undone it is rambling and unwieldy. My fear unravels and I watch it and I SEE and I let go of it. It just moves through me and out while the tree branches move in the breeze.

Maggie and I sit together all morning. In silence but completely engrossed. When the sun hangs overhead my fear trails out of me and my breath slows and my shoulders droop. I close my eyes. I am grateful that I survived that intensity.

And when I open my eyes, I am glad to be here. Period. I can feel my heart expand. My fear walls are not constricting it any longer.

A smile dances on my lips as I look over at Maggie. She is napping. In her rest, she looks completely trusting, unafraid, with no need to protect herself. I smile wider. I feel what she meant when she spoke earlier about being glad to be alive. This may be the first time in my life I have felt grateful just to be. But I feel it now, in the sun, with Maggie, on the bench in front of the tree.

I gently pick up my drawing pad and sketch a skeleton tree in ten seconds. I repeat that twenty times on the same page. My arm moves with the movement of the tree. When I am finished, I have a veritable orchard of skeleton trees. Some are excited, some are calm, all are alive.

I tear off that page and draw a full-page tree, looking every three seconds back at the tree in front of me. I shade the branches, sketch the small lines in the trunk, and draw the soil at its base. I spend time with the tree and notice every detail.

I draw four more full-page trees, each time looking less at my paper and more at the tree. On the last drawing, I am more focused on the push from my heart and I let that guide my hand. By now I know every detail of the tree. When my hand moves with its own energy it draws a tree brimming with personality. It is alive from the inside.

I do one more drawing. This time I simply put my pencil on the paper and let it go. My arm moves across the paper swiftly, surely, confidently while I keep my eyes on the tree. And in four minutes I have a tree that laughs and loves and invites me to play. There is such energy in that tree that it is fun to look at it.

A man's voice from behind my shoulder speaks, "You love that tree, don't you?"

Maggie is not on the bench and when I turn, I see no one. But I feel him. Alex is coming closer.

CHAPTER 8
AN OPEN HEART

I am in love. I had always thought that love was a response to the right person but it isn't that at all. I am in love and there is no one around. I dance a little in the living room but most of what I do isn't that much different from other weeks. I do it with a lighter heart, though, and with a gentleness that formerly escaped me.

Having my heart open feels like a waterfall. My feelings rush through my body and fall away like water rushes and falls. My joy and excitement and sadness and anger tumble through my chest and flow on. When I let my feelings move, they move quickly and they keep moving. I don't stop them or even think about them. They come and then they pass. Not maintaining fear walls releases me.

My concerns don't seem so weighty. I don't worry about the future although it is getting increasingly difficult to discern. I content myself with my immediate surroundings and with today. I arrange some wildflowers and set them on the dining room table and I clean some windows. I pull out a piece of yellow and orange paisley material I had salvaged from a garage sale and improvise a runner for my dresser. And surprise of surprises — I open a cookbook. Granted, I only look at the pictures but, still, that is a change.

While I am doing these things, Theresa sits on the window seat and watches me. She speaks not at all but her eyes don't miss a thing. She doesn't seem as far away as she was the first time I met her but she isn't the laughing person I had seen last, either. I talk to her, not expecting a response, just acknowledging her presence.

"These blue flowers are lovely, don't you think? The shade is electric against the white walls." And I putter and nest and generally enjoy a pleasant day.

After lunch I read, sitting on my bedroom floor. When I come out of the bedroom, Theresa is gone. Not thinking much of it, I unload the dishwasher and sweep the deck. This puttering is fine but I am running out of things to do.

I sit on the porch in the rocking chair in the late afternoon and Theresa appears next to me. Still not saying much, she sits and I read. As the light disappears from the yard, she asks in a little girl voice if I have ever been to the circus.

"Why, yes, of course." I am surprised. Wasn't she with me? "I liked the elephants best. They were huge but they were graceful when they stepped on a platform as the ringleader touched their front legs. Don't you remember, Theresa?"

"I remember the smell of cotton candy," she says, "so sticky that even its aroma clogged my nose."

Theresa looks into the evening as she remembers more. "And the buttery popcorn and the fresh hay mingled their aromas 'til I felt like the world was mine to inhale. And I remember the dancing ladies in their red tutus, their necks bent back in the rings that held them above us. They twirled into a blur way above the floor.

"And I remember the flying acrobats who grabbed each other's arms over the huge net, releasing one trapeze and floating for two seconds in the air while we held our breath, hoping they would find each other there in space. And they did. I guess they always do, but when we saw them we thought that this was the only time that mattered, the time we watched them, and we prayed they would connect and they did and we loved them for their bravery, for risking their lives to make us happy.

"And I remember the lions — huge, sleek, fast, beautiful beasts who leaped surefooted through blazing hoops on fire and bounded around the ring. And the goofy clowns with their ridiculous noses and their water-squirting corsages and their flapping shoes. They made us laugh.

"And outside I remember the thrill I felt when I rode on the roller coaster that was going so fast, so fast, so fast I was out of my mind with fear and excitement and I had to swallow my heart to return it to my chest.

"And when we were older, I remember my quiet joy when Grams prepared mushroom lentil soup with Italian parsley from her garden and baked dill bread and picked fat strawberries to serve us with fresh cream. The steam made the kitchen humid and my mouth water.

"But you know the memories that touched my soul? Holding a sleeping baby who didn't yet distrust, pulling a kitten onto my lap who wanted to eat and needed me to feed it, exchanging silent smiles with a stranger passing on the street. I let them touch me in my heart and it was pure and it was holy."

Theresa shifts in her seat and faces me.

"You know, Annie, you know what I really really want from you? I want you to live inside my skin for an hour, to see life the way I see it, to feel what I feel, to cry, and to laugh with me. I want you to explode in my outrage and snuggle in my pillow.

"Will you sit with me by the fire and listen and talk and tell stories of the days that are only gone in time but still live in vivid colors in our minds? Will you let your heart play with mine?"

Theresa makes my heart ache. Now I remember those times and those tastes and those smells. Where had they gone? They bring back the memory of my cat when I was a girl. Winster Bedeliah was black with white paws and I loved her and she loved me. When I would lie in the wet grass early in the morning in the backyard, she would pick up her socked feet so daintily and lie on my chest and purr while she slept and I read the clouds.

"And I remember the creek behind grandmother's house that raced in the spring but was a parched path for raccoons in August. It hid treasures — stones it had polished 'til they were smooth and gray like exotic jewels. I would gather them and pretend they were my fortune.

"And my father, the king, would say to the handsome princes from the faraway lands, 'You can only have my daughter's hand in marriage if you know how many stones there are in my kingdom.' And the princes would wander and count and come back but they never got it right. They never knew the correct number.

"And my father would tell them to go away. Then he would tell me, 'They aren't right for you, my princess. The right one will know the secret number.' And, so, my father never let me leave his kingdom.

"And I remember my first drive-in movie on the hot, sticky Midwest night when the sun had already set earlier than it did the month before and the mosquitos were small birds who visited my skin without fear and carried my blood away with them. I remember pretending to watch Alfie while I knew Jeff was looking at my face, wondering if he dared touch my cheek and how it would feel to kiss my lips. I had not kissed a boy.

"And he and I ended up in the back seat and we kissed and he touched my new breasts and I sighed and I gasped and then held my breath and then I screamed. It was such pleasure and joy and excitement and it scared me.

"So, I kept screaming and the manager directed his flashlight beam in the window and gruffly demanded to know 'What's going on?' Couldn't he guess? Wasn't that why all the kids came here? He knew it wasn't for the old movies he showed.

"And Jeff pushed his head up from the back seat and said, 'No problem, here, sir. Everything is under control.' And he was angry with me and drove me home without talking and I got out and Jeff never spoke to me again.

"'No problem, sir. Everything is under control.' And it has stayed under control. And no man has ever known the secret number. And I am still in my father's kingdom."

Theresa and I are both crying when I fall silent. She knows and I know she knows what it is like to be so afraid that I would willingly sacrifice my life rather than be disappointed one more time, rather than lose one more love. The disappointments swallowed me whole. Better that I lose my passion and my hope and my joy.

"It was Jeff that summer and Jack the next year and Bill and Dave after that and pretty soon I identified the time in my life by the man I had lost. And when I got to Glen after I had been through Harold with the loud ties and Matt with the long hair and Gerry who went nowhere without his guitar slung on his back, well by the time Glen came along, I couldn't be touched. Glen was nice and he was sweet but I knew how it would end. Why go through it?

"So, to save myself the heartache I didn't let my heart near him.

He never had a chance. And after that, I didn't, either.

"And then it was one man after another but none of them mattered and I wasn't surprised when they left. I barely noticed. I truly didn't care. Because I couldn't. I couldn't care anymore and risk being destroyed. I couldn't keep my passion with me and still walk upright through the world."

I look at Theresa as I speak these words and her eyes are wet and so soft. Her head tilts to the left and she reaches out with her long thin arms and whispers, "Oh, Annie, oh," and she holds me. She knows. She is the only person in the world who really knows what losing my passion has cost me. And she loves me. And I love her.

We hold each other and our hearts beat together.

CHAPTER 9
THE PARK

For the three nights after my talk with Theresa, I don't sleep well. My senses are open and my body buzzes, too alert for rest. After a tossing and turning night, before the sun is up, I walk to the park.

The park at dawn hums its own poetry. Cool air nips my cheeks. Leaves on the young trees sway slightly, prodded by a silent breeze. The light has no apparent source, the cloud-packed sky as opaque as a photographer's backdrop. Tiny staccato chirps of the sparrows are punctuated by the harsh claws of the giant blackbirds.

The moist air coats the play equipment with a fine mist. A red wooden adventure ship is beached in the sandlot. For twenty feet, vertical wooden slats suggest the boat's shape. A three-step ladder permits entry to a white lookout platform. A white wooden flag displays a black line drawing of a child, arms and legs outstretched.

To the left of the ship, as I look at it from my bench, are the sandlot playhouses. Two three-foot by three-foot roofed rooms on stilts stand above the sand, high enough for a ten-year-old to walk upright underneath. The two houses are connected by a blue rope spider web that hangs down to the sand.

To the left of the playhouses is the huge maze-like jungle gym, slide, and hanging bridge edifice. This child megalopolis jumps with activity after school but at this hour stillness shrouds it.

To the right of the sandlot stretch four fenced playing fields, circled by a sidewalk. Early morning walkers grind the sand from the sandlot into the sidewalk and a man on his bike holds his Labrador's leash as he pedals and the dog trots. A silent couple and a chatting pair walk past. At this hour, no woman wears make-up and no man is shaved.

We are all here in the park at the same time, but we are still in our own worlds, not yet having completely emerged from the night, not yet ready to meet and greet each other. Everyone knows why he is here and goes about his walk or jog and does not seek or expect recognition. The park in its early morning light is the intermediate point between our solitary slumber and full alertness.

These dawn moments are suspended, not part of the mystery of the night or the productivity of the day. And I feel suspended, too. I realize yet another time that I can't live the life I've known and I don't know what is coming.

The anxiety from that realization pushes my legs to walk to the north end of the playing fields. I sit at the picnic table near the basketball courts. Now what? I feel like I don't belong anywhere in the world. It's not a bad not-belonging, just a sense of un-tetheredness.

The sun punches through the cloud wall and inches up the sky. Children walk with their mothers to the elementary school on the south side of the park. Some hold hands but most don't, walking silently. This is what they do every day. They are on track and, as the day unfolds, they know what it will bring.

I don't know anything.

Since I don't know what to do, I sit here with my back to the basketball courts, looking across the four baseball fields. It's funny how after you let go of what you thought was important, life is actually easier to accept than when you thought there was still a chance that your old ways would work a bit longer and you're trying to hold on. There is no doubt in my mind that my old way is gone forever. And, really, I haven't lost everything. I still have my condo which, thankfully, is paid for. That is a huge comfort. I will always have a home.

Now the question remains, Can I construct a home inside me?

How am I going to live in a way that is life-giving?

With the children in school, the moms walk home and the park settles into its second quiet time of the morning. One man rifles through the trash barrel on the east side of the fence by the bathrooms, filling his green plastic bag with pop cans. A grandmother pushes a baby in a stroller. And here I am.

I peel off my sweatshirt. And I sit and look. I look at the park but what I see is my own blank canvas. I can paint any scene I want for my next forty-plus years. What will I be glad I've done after I'm dead? Not making money. I've known success in business but I don't feel pulled to keep doing that. The rewards seem superficial when I think about eternity.

Even being in love well, which I have never done, doesn't contribute to my sense of being a strong independent woman. I have given myself away for love which has hurt me badly. I have betrayed myself. I don't need to focus on any other person. It doesn't serve me. My commitment has to be to the deepest parts of myself. What will answer my post-death question satisfactorily, and the only thing I can come up with sitting here on the picnic table is to be as completely myself as I can be. Not to live in response to fear or to act compulsively. I don't want to go through my days one after another and wake up and find I'm dead and say, where did my time go? No, I want to choose consciously.

"That's a nifty thought, sweetie," and before I turn around, I know Hannah is here. She sports a royal blue jogging suit with red and green intertwining circles across her shoulders. Her cap matches her jacket. She looks like an older Nordie's shopper who buys her outfits whole.

"Hey, Hannah, I'm glad you're here. I'm reconstructing my life."

"You're thinking maybe you can design a new existence to fit a new you?"

"Yes, and I have some ideas about what I want and what I can forget. For instance, it's..." and in Hannah's fashion, she snorts her disdain and cuts me off.

"Annie, what will it take to pry you loose from your

interminable abominable thinking? Don't you ever get tired of that wheel spinning in your brain? Over and over and over and over. Now this. No, now

that. And you race from one solution to another. Annie, get this: it isn't about solutions. There isn't a problem. This is your life. The only question is, are you willing to truly live it?"

"Well, sure, yes, of course, there's no doubt about that..."

"Your words are great but you aren't off the what-do-you-call-those little things the rats run around on? You know what I mean... well, your mind has its own whatever-that-is and it's burning up the rubber going around and around and around and I'm getting dizzy. Get off it. Just get off the whole thing."

As usual, I didn't follow Hannah very precisely. How could anyone follow that explanation precisely?

"See, Anne, don't worry about precise. This isn't a job to be done right. Theresa showed you your passion. Living your life with a commitment to your passion is really your only choice now. Do you want that or not? It's up to you."

"Of course, I want that." I am annoyed again as I usually am when I feel put on the spot by Hannah. She doesn't need to be so impatient. Haven't I come a very, very long way since that night, months ago, when I first met her?

"Chill, sweets," Hannah admonishes me. "There is no enemy. And there is no problem. Just this marvelous opportunity you have. So, what are you going to do with your next half-lifetime?"

I know better than to answer. This is a Hannah question, one for which she already has a response, a question that doesn't need or welcome a reply from me. So, I wait, and not very long before she speaks again.

"You see, Annie, you see, it's like this. Now you can go this way," and she draws an invisible straight path on the picnic table," or you can jump off the edge. "Well, it's your choice but really I feel like I should offer my two cents and I am here to tell you that staying on top of the table is no way to spend your time."

I never have to guess where I stand with Hannah. She isn't subtle but she is honest and forthright and frank. And I know that how I spend my second half of life isn't my decision totally. I had prayed for direction and Hannah is here and I have to acknowledge that she is a voice of mine, strange as that often seems. I have to listen to her.

She continues without looking at me. "Now when you jump off the edge," and her fingers walked off the picnic table, "well, Annie, that's when your real life begins."

"That's not when I get squashed and given up for crazy?" I am playing with her but she isn't looking at me and she doesn't see my smile.

"No. No, you don't ever have to worry about that. Well, maybe the crazy part. Yes, sometimes that may happen but don't let it bother you." I smile more broadly, thinking about how many thousands and millions of people would say that Hannah is nuts. Her total lack of self-consciousness warms my heart and I put my arm around her.

"It's you and me, Hannah," I announce jovially and she looks at me, a bit surprised.

"Why, yes," and she's quiet. But only for a minute.

"That is true but I'm not sure you really get totally what that means yet."

I'm not going to worry that I don't, I think. Life is coming at me pretty fast. I'm satisfied to just keep up.

"OK, Hannah, tell me what that means. I'm all yours."

She hesitates and looks across the playing fields. Perhaps she is planning her thoughts. As soon as I think that, I laugh. Nothing about Hannah is planned. She looks at me quizzically in response to my laugh before she speaks in a low voice.

"Annie, I want you to listen very carefully and to think about what I am saying. This is the most important step you will ever take."

"You got it, Hannah."

"No, really, I want you to say goodbye to everything you've ever known. Most of all to your mind. I want you to let it float away."

"I can feel that happen even as we speak," I retort more sincerely than I wish were true.

"And then I want you to trust. Don't do anything, don't plan anything, don't even think anything. Surrender and trust. You'll be led."

"How will I know?"

And Hannah is gone. Just like her — when I want specifics she's nowhere around. So, I sit and I wait and I try not to think. At least when I catch myself thinking, I stop.

It's early afternoon but I still don't know what to do. I sit and I walk and I stretch a bit on top of the picnic table and I am totally confused and lost. But it's a lovely day to be confused and lost. So, I enjoy the sun and the breeze. And pretty soon I am asleep in the grass.

In my dream, I am hiking along a path beside a small river. There is no bank, only boulders that look like they have fallen from the side of the mountain. I need to cross the river, I don't know why, and I can't find a way across. The water is too swift. Even on the other side, there are only more huge granite rocks. I'm baffled.

A white parachute drifts down from the sky and deposits a young, slender dark-haired man on a rock on the other side of the river. "Just fly," he invites me and he extends his arm.

It is Alex but I am annoyed. I can't fly. I can't move in any direction.

"Just fly," he repeats and I shrug my shoulders.

"I need a bridge. I can't fly," I respond and he fades away. I am left alone among the rocks next to the river I don't dare cross.

I awaken with a start and, before I open my eyes, I recognize that I'm in a foul mood.

"Why do you people do this to me?" I say aloud with my eyes closed. A man laughs.

"Apparently, you've gotten your marching orders."

"Marching I can do. My orders are to fly." And I look at the man. He's at least 80 with a long white and gray beard and wire-rimmed glasses. The lines extending from his eyes tell me that he has laughed a hundred thousand times. His face, worn and tough, is also gentle. I feel comfortable with him already.

"Ah, flying. Yes, I remember that one," and his head falls back and he laughs again. "Yes, you'll have fun with that."

"Fun? I have no idea what to do. I can't fly. No human can fly."

"Oh, well now, missy," and he crosses his legs, "don't be so sure of that. There is more we can do than has ever been told. And anyway, it doesn't matter what anyone else has done. This is your time." He sits back, leaning against the table and I stand up and sit on the bench two feet from him. He chuckles as he strokes his beard.

"I know and I _am_ open but I didn't think I would be asked to fly. How can I possibly do that?"

"I think the question really is how can you not?" His eyes twinkle, his cheeks puff into two red balls on the ends of a huge grin, and he evaporates. His laugh lingers in the air after he is gone.

CHAPTER 10
FLYING

Flying sounds good. It also sounds efficient. Saves wear and tear on shoes. I don't know what makes me trust the old man but I do, completely, and he had said I can't not fly. So, that is that. I am going to fly. I just don't know how. But Hannah has taught me not to worry about specifics.

The next day is a two-client day in the office — at least I have two clients scheduled. Any more I don't count on anything actually happening as it is planned. I am early and I sit at my desk sorting the mail. Lots of junk. But one flyer that intrigues me. GLIDE TO HEAVEN it announces. A glider port has opened near my home and they are offering introductory ground instruction lessons free every Saturday morning at 9:30. I hear the old man's laugh and I know I must go. Within ten minutes I have reserved my place for this Saturday.

The glider port, south of my home on the other side of the state reserve, sits on the cliffs three hundred and fifty feet directly above the beach. From my condo a mile north of the glider port I can drive inland half a mile, circle the state reserve, and drive into the glider port from the south. Or I can walk the mile through the reserve, closed to cars. I choose the latter.

I walked up the steep hill and entered the north gate of the reserve. The oldest paved road in the county, unused by cars for decades now, meanders through the natural habitat designated a protected environment. Although I can hear traffic sounds from the freeway below me to the east, I am in a different world here.

Between the road and the ocean, a quarter mile to my right, grow layers upon layers upon layers of indigenous bushes and plants in a dozen shades of green. The constant breeze from the ocean carries the scents of sage, lemonade berries, and pine needles. Walking through the reserve I don't forget that I am on my way to an appointment. But I promise myself that I will come back here to enjoy the serenity when I can linger.

I walk between the narrow posts at the south end of the park and out of the reserve. The road continues through a low-cut field which turns into a huge dirt parking area. At the far end of the parking lot is the glider port. There is fifteen times as much room for cars as there is on the mound from which the drivers-turned-pilots take flight. The "No Spectators Beyond This Point" sign restricts access to the mound to the committed few who will actually walk off the edge of the cliff.

The cliffs were been formed by erosion of sandstone over thousands of years. They drop abruptly to the beach as though the westernmost land had been sliced away and carried off by the ocean. Rough reddish-brown ridges channeling thousands of vertical river beds race down the face of the cliffs. From close range, the sandstone looks like it will crumble in a fierce rain, as indeed it does during our once-a-decade thunderstorms. "Unstable" and "Dangerous" signs are posted over the cliffs; climbing is forbidden. Flying is OK.

As I walk west up the hill to the mound of the glider port, I see that the ocean in the background is gorgeous today. In the foreground at a small table across from the mound are two men talking.

The one facing the mound wearing sunglasses greets me as I approach them. "You're Anne? I'm David. Glad to have you. This morning it's just you and Barry."

I shake hands with Barry, younger than I am, and grinning as widely as his cheek muscles allow. I feel his excitement in the strong grip of his handshake. He has a mustache and the currently popular long-hair-on-top, short-on-the-sides cut. His brown eyes dance. He tells us that he is a dentist but that he does some form of extreme sport on the weekends.

"Filling cavities and extracting wisdom teeth is a pretty small world. I want more on my own time. Flying can take me places I can't go any other way." And he smiles. I am excited for him.

David takes off his sunglasses and his sky-blue eyes are steady in their gaze and penetrating. His short curly hair is prematurely white. He has the air of an aging hippie — loose, trusting, and comfortable, but with a commitment to his work and his life. A slight drawl when he speaks betrays a childhood in a southern state.

When David asks me why I am here, I stammer, "I don't know." His laugh gives me a cover and I quickly continue. "I'm curious. I received a flyer and I want to know what's going on here." Why do I feel foolish in that adolescent way I had hoped I had outgrown? Fortunately, David is into the spiel he must have given 400 hundred times before and the spotlight is off me.

"When I was a kid, I was so scared of heights that I climbed steps on my knees until I was eight," he explains. "After I graduated from high school, I didn't want to live with fear anymore and, besides, it wasn't macho." He laughs as though macho were something he aspired to at a younger age.

"I wanted more," and he nods towards Barry. "I knew life wasn't just school and football games but I didn't know what else there was. When I moved out here, I fell in love with hang gliding. In those days the hang gliders were big and clumsy and there were no regulations. Now they are sleeker but a few years ago I tried paragliding and I haven't flown any other way since."

He speaks of hang gliding and paragliding as flying. My skin shivers.

Paragliding, I learned, is flying with a nylon parachute,

thirty-five feet long horizontally over the pilot and five feet from front to back. David motions to the brightly colored canopies in the sky. There are dozens of lines that permit the pilot, sitting in a harness, to manipulate the canopy. From a distance I cannot see the lines; to me, the paragliders look like rainbows over black dots.

"Paragliding is flying like a bird," David continues. "Hang gliding is flying like a plane. The hang glider under his fiberglass sails goes faster than the paraglider but isn't as graceful. The paraglider feels his connection to the wind more. He pulls toggles to direct his chute and he moves on the wind in the same way a bird does.

"When I began paragliding, I learned to move like the wind and to read the sky. I learned that an overcast sky in the morning often leads to sun and good wind in the afternoon. When the sun comes out, the wind picks up.

"I learned to read the clouds — the high cirrus clouds which are so beautiful to see are not always good for soaring. They sit on top of a high-pressure area which is bad for gliders. The air underneath them doesn't move.

"But the puffy cumulus clouds, like those," and he points to the western horizon, "they make for good flying. They're over updrafts that will carry you into the sky. You can see what kind of clouds are coming in and know what that will mean for flying.

"When I see a sky with cumulus clouds on the western horizon, I know there will be good flying in an hour. When the sky is completely clear, it's better to wait for the early evening glass off." He notices my glassed-off stare and explains.

"At the end of the day, the ground heating slows down. The ocean temperature is always the same, so as the ground cools the ocean temperature predominates. Even though there may not be wind, the airflow is strong. We call it 'magic air.'

"When the airflow comes from the ocean into the cliffs and all the air rises at the same rate — it's called a laminar current — that's the best for beginning flyers — no surprises, easy to glide.

"When you are inland and flying over asphalt or dark ground

cover that has heated during the day, it causes the air to warm and rise," he raises his hands together, "creating thermal lift. The heat carries the air straight up. Just before you hit a thermal, there's a bump and you drop a bit and then you catch the updraft, and you can spiral up 1000 feet a minute." He looks heavenward and is not with us for a few seconds. He sees something we can't.

"And that gives just a great ride." He laughs and he is back.

David knows what I want to learn and the longer he talks, the surer I am that he is the person to teach me. I suspect that what I will learn is more than paragliding.

"When you fly," he continues with a bit more focus, "You're part of the sky and the wind. When the gliders are up there," and he gestures to the sky which holds four gliders as he speaks, "it doesn't matter who you are or what you wear on Monday morning. Money doesn't count. It's only about listening to the wind and working with it and letting it move you.

"And after you've been up there, you always look at the sky and wish you were back. Paragliding is the most passionate, intense experience you can have." His expression changes from wistful to mischievous.

"If our wives knew how much we love flying — we love it more than <u>anything</u> — we'd be in big trouble." We all laugh. This is exactly where I need to be.

I sign up for a tandem paragliding lesson. Tandem flights are actually illegal except for those with instructors licensed by the United States Hang Gliding Association through a special exemption granted by the Federal Aviation Administration. David is one of the licensed few.

If any licensed instructor anywhere in the U.S. injures or kills a client during a tandem lesson, all instructors lose the privilege of flying tandem. That's a lot of pressure on them to make it safe and, so far, no one has been hurt.

If David takes me flying tandem and we crash and die, he has more to lose than I do. I would simply be dead, but not only would he be dead, he would have forfeited the right of all U.S. instructors to offer tandem flights and they would be furious with him. I find this piece of information oddly comforting. No risk for me, I think, only the opportunity to soar. I have to fly.

Before I can even walk onto the mound I must sign three forms — I will not sue regardless of what happens. I am responsible for any injury I may sustain and I will not make a claim. I voluntarily assume all risks and hold the glider port responsible for none even if they are caused in whole or part by the equipment. I hold my left side and bring Hannah's attention to the last. I can feel her harrumph up my spine. I signed three times.

Signing the requisite forms buys me entrance to the mound. The wind is stronger here than just a few feet back in the parking lot. One man, already on the mound, flies a small radio-controlled plane over the edge of the cliffs.

David lays our pink chute out on the ground. Our only choice is how to get the chute overhead and carry us.

There are two kinds of launches in paragliding — the forward lunge in which the paraglider faces the wind with the chute at his back and runs into it. This method is preferable on light wind days. When the pilot moves forward at five to eight mph, he creates the needed airflow over and under the canopy for the lift and take-off.

Because the wind off the ocean is so predictable, blowing steadily at ten mph, David chooses approach #2: the reverse launch. It requires less exertion and provides the pilot with more "visual input," as he phrases it. With the chute lying on the ground the pilot backs into the wind. The pilot can see the chute every minute, checking the lines and noting the fullness of the canopy as it rises.

We are fifth in line to launch off the side of the cliff and as we wait David talks with me about what he has learned from paragliding. "After I had flown a while I realized that paragliding isn't just a sport; it's a way of life. When I wasn't flying, I watched myself moving over and around obstacles, like the wind moves over the chute.

"It's like the martial art of aikido — I learned to use the force of what is around me to carry me, not to fight it but rather to flow with it. I felt connected to everything and I was willing to be a part of it all. I didn't need to blaze my own trail and make my own mark but I did need to know my place among the forces around me which are much, much, much bigger than I am.

"Flying has taught me humility and respect. I have so much respect for nature — the wind playing off the earth and the ocean. From the birds I have learned to soar — to trust the wind but to be ready to shift with every bump that demands that I change my direction or my altitude. I've learned to let the wind carry me and not to be determined about what is going to happen and where I'll end up. Soaring is a gift, the art of understanding my connection with nature and with the wind.

"In teaching paragliding, I have learned to dial into each person who is taking a lesson — sensing where she is, what she wants, what she can handle. One day last month a young very heavy woman came out and wanted to make a tandem flight. We usually discourage overweight flyers because in tandem flight it is very hard to control the chute with them in the harness.

"But I looked at her and I realized that she was handicapped, that because of her weight, she has missed lots of neat experiences. I said to myself, I am going to make sure she flies this one time.

"She was so excited when we were up and, yes, it was a lot of work for me, but I was glad to share the gift of free flight with her. She had never experienced her body defying the earth's gravitational pull. Gravity for her must have confined her emotionally in addition to her obvious physical limitations.

"As I sat behind her in my harness, I could feel something in her body float away. The only word she spoke when we were in the air was 'Freedom.' The wind lifting her into the heavens was probably the freest she had felt in her life. Other than that simple word — freedom — she was silent throughout the whole flight.

"I could see that she was crying with the wind on her face. When we landed, the tears didn't stop streaming down her cheeks. She didn't say much. She just pulled me down and gave me a peck on the cheek and thanked me. She said I'd never know how much it meant to her.

"To be able to give another human that experience, to sense her limitations and to say, 'I won't let that stop me... I can show her some part of her soul that she hasn't seen before,' Well, that's worth everything.

"I've learned about love from paragliding. Love is when you accept what is there in front of you and you are one with it."

CHAPTER 11
MAGIC

In minutes it is our turn and David springs into action. He is all business as he untangles the five dozen lines between the canopy on the ground and the toggles on his harness. I watch, surprisingly calm and trusting, waiting to be told when to move.

David adjusts the straps of my harness around my legs and my waist. In flight, I will be sitting in the seat of my harness attached to him behind me sitting in his harness controlling the canopy with the toggles. But to launch he faces the canopy lying on the ground with his back to me as I face the cliff. With a wind of 10 mph, I lean forward and pull into it but can't move.

Behind me David pulls on the lines connecting the canopy to his harness as the wind rushes into it, raising it a foot from the ground. He turns around so that he is facing my back and connects his harness and the canopy to my harness with large hooks on the straps above my shoulders. He announces, "OK, we're off. Walk to the edge." The canopy rises overhead easily with both of us facing the ocean and we are lifted off the ground even before we reach the edge of the cliff.

I am in the sky and I'm not working at staying aloft. I'm not working at anything. Even thinking seems blasphemous here. This is a different world in which nothing is required of me except to be part of the sky. I feel free.

The birds fly farther out over the ocean while we stay above or slightly west of the cliffs. I'm not aware of the updrafts or the shifts in the wind but David mentions them as he adjusts the canopy. We look down on the beach and the houses farther south on the cliff. From this perspective, the little structures seem insignificant. The colors of the sky and the ocean and the sand and the grass are bolder and clearer than I have ever seen blues and greens and tans.

It is exhilarating, but mostly it is right. I have reunited with something inside myself, something natural and easy. Something that has been missing that I didn't even realize was gone. Something that is more than the me I know. I find a part of my soul I had lost. And when I find it, I find peace. A profound, deep-in- the-cells-of-my-body peace. And I know that I don't ever want to lose that peace.

For the first time in my life, I have a sense of being just fine. It is an acceptance of myself. This is how I was always meant to live but, in my anxiety, to construct the "right" life I had lost it. It is very good to have it back.

I can feel something in me release and dissipate. Something stiff that helped me walk through the world appropriately and look professional, but something that is artificial and that I don't need here. And I laugh again. I am more me in the sky than I ever have been on the ground.

David turns us around and we head in the opposite direction. He says, "Did you notice that? The wind just shifted." I noticed nothing. I am lost in rapture. This world is new and familiar at the same time. However, the cliffs are getting closer and we are losing altitude.

"Don't leave us now, Wind Gods," David prays. "Keep us up."

But the Wind Gods are unresponsive and withdraw their favors. We gently and gracefully float down. In two minutes, I slide out of my harness for a soft landing on the beach. And, as quickly as we were in the sky, we were back on the earth. But now it feels awkward to walk on solid ground.

"The winds forsake us sometimes and we just have to go with it." David is amused and I am impressed with his flexibility. A whole drama of diminishing wind currents had occurred and I hadn't noticed.

We fold the chute and pack it and climb up the cliffs. I thank David and walk back through the reserve. What I had just experienced preoccupies me and I'm not aware of the plants and the scents.

I follow the last trail at the north end, High Point Trail, as it veers off the main road to the right. It is only 60 feet long, curving up and around a small hill, ending under a spreading old pine. A log cut in half is now a bench I claim. I need to sit and be still to allow the jumble inside me to settle. My flight had been only ten minutes long but already I knew that its effects would be with me forever.

I breathe the piney air without noticing it or the squirrels or the ant freeway at my feet. I am somewhere else. My body has come down from the sky but my heart hasn't. I know then that I can't resume my day-in-day-out way of being me.

A deep place in my soul has been touched, arousing a part of me that hasn't fully been born until now. I experienced magic. I flew in the air. I was smiled upon by the gods, even if they took their winds away too soon.

Not only could I fly and be safe, by flying I had found myself. I wasn't expecting flying to make me solid on the inside but it did. More than anything else I had ever done. I felt compact in my chest and totally without fear about being me.

As I sit under that pine tree, I feel a new confidence about living in a way that is completely my own. I don't know what that means exactly but I trust myself. I know that I will now, finally, be living on my own terms. Not intimidated, not pleasing, not fearful, not trying to predict the future, not second-guessing someone else, not needing anyone to validate me or even to walk with me, and not trying to fit in. I have found myself by leaving the ground.

And all it took was surrender — letting go of my expectations and forgetting what I knew. What I had experienced in the sky was a connection. Just as David said, I was connected to the wind and through the wind to the ocean and without the wind to the ground. I was moved by the air in response to the shifts in land and ocean temperature. It was totally unlike anything I had ever experienced. I was in a world I couldn't see and I fit just fine.

I was also connected to parts of me I had forgotten. Flying required a childlike trust I hadn't allowed myself for decades. That much vulnerability wasn't part of my adult life. I trusted David to guide our flight but we both trusted the wind to carry us. I may have felt that trust in infancy but it had been buried for so long that I had forgotten it was in me. Being in the sky had taken me deeper into myself than I had been for a long long time.

"Thank you," I whisper to the heavens. "Thank you."

It doesn't surprise me when Alex sits down on the log bench to my right. His very dark hair is sprinkled with gray and his khaki pants are wrinkled. Standing he is six feet tall, but when he sits, he could be my twin. Granted, a twin who has seen the inside of a gym for many more hours than I have. His chest and arms are thick but he has my blue eyes and my straight nose.

"I've had the most amazing morning," I tell him (needlessly) and he smiles gently.

"My anxiety motor switched off. I hadn't known I had lived with it, it was so subtle. And I was filled with peace. I had nothing to prove or to disprove. There wasn't any particular way I had to be. Just a very very deep knowing that who I was at that moment and how I was right then were perfectly fine. There wasn't a struggle and there wasn't a goal and there wasn't a problem. I just was. And that was enough.

"Some part of my heart that had been missing was back in place.

I felt whole." I am gushing but I can't stop myself.

"Being in the sky was a totally different experience of being, just being. It was such a privilege to be there, Alex. The birds around me were just being, the ocean was just being, the wind was being itself. And I was part of it all. Just by being. It was sacred and, when I respectfully took my place in it, I was scared, too. And the sacredness was inside me as well. Alex, I've found the magic I've always searched for. I flew in the sky and reached a part of me I didn't remember."

I am very sure that the flight was my teacher, not simply a drug that provides a temporary fix. The thrill was remarkable but the magic is mine forever.

Alex puts his arm around my shoulder and his compassion floods me.

"And you learned something else, too," he offers quietly. I look at him and he continues.

"You opened yourself to partnership. Partnership with the life around you. You cooperated with life and let it teach you.

"Partnership has always been available to you but you had to welcome it. When you did, not only were you guided and carried, you found yourself."

"Yes, I felt that."

"And you're right. You are magic. The magic is inside you. It's also in the sky and the wind and in every other person. But you can connect to it, be one with it when you let go and allow yourself to be carried. Don't ever forget that you are magic."

I squeeze his hand and gaze over the bushes toward the ocean. I feel like a fog has lifted and I am seeing the earth I thought I knew clearly for the first time. I hold Alex's hand so tightly in my lap until I realize I might be hurting him. When I look over to ask, he is gone. But I can still feel his hand in mine.

CHAPTER 12
PARTNERSHIP

Over the next few weeks, I practice partnership. During the day when I need to make a decision — Do I have time to run one more errand or should I stay put? — I ask and I wait. Within seconds I feel the answer in my body — just a sense of what is right for me. There isn't a pattern to the "responses" I receive — they aren't always yes's or no's. I notice that whenever I ask, I am answered and that the answer always works out well. I learn to trust my unseen partner.

My life takes on a gentle quality. Being in partnership is far more important than doing any specific thing. When I am in partnership I listen and I speak and I listen again. I'm in a dialogue. I am recognized and acknowledged. I feel understood. I am never alone.

Whatever I want to do, I talk over first. (I'm afraid I would be diagnosed schizophrenic if I share this information with my colleagues.) By relying on my partnership dialogue for direction and to make decisions, I grow calm.

In the evenings I practice partnership with Alex. I find him sitting in the living room when I come in or leaning against the kitchen counter when I wash the dishes. We talk about my concerns of the day but he always brings our conversation, wherever it starts, back to personal power. He is determined that I be aware of my power and move into it. I ask him why that is so important.

"You're not you without it. You haven't grown into your life if you're not living from your power."

"Is that passion?"

"Passion is one aspect of living from your power but power is all-encompassing. Your power comes from your soul. It is the essence of who you are. When you live in your head or in reaction to what is around you, you're not living your own life. Only when you are in your power do you know what is right for you. And that's your job — to be yourself fully and never to escape being yourself. Not with work or being nice or helping others or keeping yourself distracted."

I am offended. "I haven't done that for a while now. If you're telling me to do something, differently tell me what that is."

"I want you to be you from the inside of the centermost cell in your body. I want you to be so focused on that voice from way inside you that you don't think about anything else. You say that you're magic, well, let your magic lead you even deeper.

"When you listen to that voice in your center you're honoring it but you're also treating it as though it were separate. Your attitude toward it is one of respect more than one of ownership. It's you, yes, but it's more you than your mind is, so you have to listen and let it show you what it wants. Always be open to that voice from your deepest center."

"OK" seems an inadequate response to such ardent direction so I am silent. Within five minutes Alex is restless, pacing in front of the fireplace, and thrusting his hands in and out of his pockets.

"Come on," he says, "Let's go to the trail. There's something you need to hear."

We walk to the reserve and to the bench on High Point Trail. I think of it as our spot, Alex's and mine. We sit looking over the bushes and the cacti toward the ocean with the sun setting into it. Alex is still restless.

"OK," I say, "I'm all ears."

"An interesting phrase. So, use them. Listen. What do you hear?" Alex seems to strain to pull something out of the air. I wait.

These days I am better at waiting than I have ever been.

"Do you hear that?" Alex asks me as he tilts his head. I presume his question is rhetorical rather than one requiring a considered response from me, so, noncommittally and out of habit, I say, "Hmmm."

"No, really, listen." He is intent on pulling some sound out of the air but I am baffled. Whatever it is I am supposed to hear eludes me.

"Did you hear it that time?"

There is nothing to hear. Nothing has happened. I am getting impatient.

With a touch of exasperation in his voice, Alex instructs me, "You need to concentrate and let go of your mind. Allow yourself to be carried. Use your seeing. Fly while you're sitting here, Anne." And he closes his eyes.

This is bizarre.

"OK, Alex," I say hoping he won't notice how uninvolved I am. I want to cooperate but I am lost.

After two minutes he opens his eyes and looks at me. "Anne, pay attention. You're pushing him away!"

"Who is it, Alex, and how am I pushing whomever it is away?" Alex is in a place I can't reach.

"Anne, we're losing it! You've got to help me . . . oh, no, it's gone."

"Huh?" Again, I feel like a bystander as I have so many times these last months. I don't know what is happening. Is this how babies feel, I wonder. I feel like a baby in a world I don't understand.

"We missed it. You've got to concentrate, Anne. Really focus and welcome him."

I demand to be let in on the secret. "Who, Alex? Who are you talking about? Who is this mystery figure? What is going on?"

Alex sighs. "Come on, we don't need to stay here any longer. We'll come back tomorrow."

And he stands up and walks back down the trail without even a nod. By the time I reach the bottom, he is gone. Alice in Wonderland comes to mind. This is getting curious and more curious.

The next day at the same time I feel a tug to go to the trail and I go by myself, finding Alex already sitting on the bench as I approach. Before I can greet him, he silences me with his raised hand, the same gesture Hannah uses. He doesn't look at me. His expression is the same as yesterday — peering into the air, searching. I sit quietly next to him until I am called on.

"Be very serious today, Anne. Listen closely. It's happening right now. Do you hear it?"

I close my eyes; that helps me focus. I hear a small voice, a baby's voice but it isn't a voice to hear as much as a voice to feel and to recognize. I can feel the baby in my bones. And I know what he wants from me. He wants me to cherish him. I keep my eyes closed and I focus on him and I listen.

He wants me to love him, protect him, and to put him first.

But when I open my eyes the whole experience vanishes.

Alex sighs irritably and concedes, "At least you heard him. He's yours. There is so much more you need to hear from him but at least it's established that he's yours and he has your attention. That's what counts."

"Who is he?"

But Alex has vanished.

I sit under the pine tree for a few more minutes and look around. It is getting dark. The day had been warm but the evening is pleasantly cool. The humidity, unusual for September, subsides for the first time in a few days and it's comfortable to be outside. The sunset sky is clouded and hazy. The muted glow of day turning into night is enchanting.

Some say this reserve was an Indian holy center hundreds of years ago. Small tribes would come for three or four days, hunt, pay homage to their spirits, and leave. No one has ever lived on this land, according to legend, but many people have traveled through here.

I can believe that was true. Something about this place is still holy. And, as I had done in the sky, I immersed myself in the holiness that exists around me. I close my eyes and I breathe. I feel my feet on the ground and invite whatever is pulsing in the ground to come into me. I can use some holiness, I think.

I need to be careful about my thoughts and now I wonder why I didn't know that already, with all the times Hannah had read them, but here I am saying offhandedly, "Holiness, come into me." I shouldn't have been surprised when it did but, of course, I am. A force like a small dam breaking rushes through my legs and into my chest. I think I am lifted up, off the bench, but when I open my eyes nothing looks different.

So, I close them again and a warm torrent races through my limbs, around my head, and into my heart. It circles faster and faster in my heart, becoming a dot. And then the dot pops. The baby is here in my heart, laughing.

I laugh when I see him. He is 9 or 10 months old, sturdy, and pink. His eyes are happy and he is attentive to me. He doesn't talk but I hear the same wish I heard from him before — cherish me, love me, protect me. I am yours.

What is this, I think to myself. He's a cutie but how can he be mine?

I'm yours, he repeats with his telepathic communication. Love me. I'm going to call you Robbie, I say, sending my thoughts to him.

Is that OK?

Love me and protect me, he says. I want to hold him. I can feel how heavy he would be if I placed him on my lap. He is past the fragile stage that has always scared me about tiny babies and he is a little person with a personality and his own wishes.

Love me and protect me, he repeats in his unspoken language.

It isn't a decision. My heart swells and I don't have to think about it. I already love Robbie and I will protect him however he needs. I feel him nestled inside my heart. He is mine and I know that forever he will be a part of me.

I walk back home with Robbie securely in my heart and the next day I start cooking.

CHAPTER 13
COOKING

When I consider cooking I think about Hannah. Lately, I don't see her and talk to her as much as I feel her. Her presence is very real but it is inside me, in my body. I think that she will be pleased by my new culinary interest.

I walk into the kitchen and announce, "Here I am. Tell me what to do, Hannah." I hope that she will dictate and I can simply follow her directives. "I'm ready," I say and I wait.

I feel pulled to take out my cookbooks. I want to be told precisely what steps to take to create a meal but instead, I am led to read the information I already have.

Over the years I have accumulated twenty-three cookbooks, from the Betty Crocker 60's vintage to the specialized Williams Sonoma picture books. Mostly they are gifts from well-meaning friends who think that my block to cooking is simply a lack of information. This morning, I looked through all the books and read about salads.

Salads are a good place to start, I think. There's a limited amount that can go wrong. So, I read the tips for making salads interesting.

The first hint is to vary the textures of the greens in a salad. I thought lettuce was iceberg lettuce. (Too many years of eating crunchy salted peanut butter.) But there are eighteen kinds of greens listed among the cookbooks I browse and these authors have actually categorized the greens according to color, texture, and flavor. Amazing.

I can handle this, I tell myself, so I make my shopping list — arugula, Belgian endive, and Bibb lettuce. I might as well start at the beginning of the alphabet and try everything in an orderly fashion. I am experimenting in a new arena but I use my old organized m.o.

Then colors need to differ. Tomatoes, especially the firm Roma tomatoes, offer color contrast without making the salad runny. Red peppers can be de-seeded, I learn, by cutting off the lower third and pushing the stem with the seeds attached through. Diced jicama accents the greens with a nice touch of off-white.

Adding shredded cabbage to greens complements them both in texture and color so I pick up some cabbage, too. However, when one cookbook suggests peeling broccoli stems to get the crunchiness without the tough outer skin, I close it. That is my limit — peeling broccoli. But I have learned a lot anyway. On day one of my new life as a cook I make salad. Another helpful hint teaches me to cover it with a moistened paper towel in the fridge to keep it crisp.

I am so pleased with myself.

I have a beautiful salad in the refrigerator and it has only taken six hours including cookbook consultations, grocery shopping, and clean up. I have learned about combining greens, but mostly I have learned about taking time.

Cooking has never seemed a time-worthy enterprise to me, but today it is. I rinse and pat the lettuce leaves and I chop vegetables carefully and I don't hurry to get anywhere else. Nothing is more important than making that salad.

Hannah has been with me every minute. And, so has Robbie. I can feel their presence. They are rooting for me and I am "cooking" with them in mind.

The next smallest step I can take after green salad is pasta salad. I learned that when I cook the noodles, I shouldn't rinse them in cold water in a colander but simply drain them and immerse them immediately in salad dressing. That way as they cool, they absorb the dressing which is the flavor for the salad.

And never chill pasta salad. Let it stand on the countertop in the dressing to cool to room temperature. Add more dressing when the vegetables are combined after an hour. Don't prepare pasta salad more than two hours before it is served.

I hadn't known that. Interesting. Day two of my life as a cook is devoted to pasta salad.

Pasta salad introduces me to garlic. When I read about garlic and pressing garlic, I found what I presume to be a garlic press that I had been given some time in the last two decades. I resurrect it from the back of a drawer of here-to-fore extraneous cooking implements and discard its very old, very dusty plastic wrapper. I place the garlic where I think the working side of the garlic press is — on top of all the little points sticking up — and I squeeze. The garlic sticks to the base of the points and I can't easily remove it. My fingernails reek of garlic for days.

Is this what garlic pressing is about? I doubt that Martha Stewart has garlic fingernails.

Back to the cookbooks. I learned that you use the flat side of the garlic press and that some chefs use the side of a knife to press garlic against a cutting board before slicing it ever so thinly. Those little pointy spikes I had identified as the working element of the technologically confounding instrument exist only to push the garlic through the little tiny holes from the other side after the liquid has been pressed out. A revelation.

Step three is obviously soup. I am already acquainted with garlic so I choose a recipe with garlic as the only seasoning. The lists in some recipes of a dozen spices, each used by the teaspoonful, seem way too complicated for me, so I choose the simplest recipes.

First, I make black bean and eggplant soup. I did soak the beans overnight but I can't wait for the eggplant to "sweat" so it goes into the pot in dry chunks. The soup turns out surprisingly well with a basic and earthy flavor from five cloves of garlic.

And my time is way down. I am into and out of the kitchen in under four hours. Efficiency combines with creativity. And several dinners in the freezer to boot. I am getting it.

My minestrone with green beans, white beans, carrots, zucchini, and pasta is memorable. Making it takes a little over three hours, adding a few chopped vegetables each hour. The minestrone is full of textures, colors, and tastes and the garden aroma fills my condo for two days.

Aroma is an important aspect of cooking and eating, I realize. In a different context years ago, I learned that the olfactory centers in the brain are primitive, far older than the parts of the brain that process language and logical thought. I have lived in those latter parts of my brain for so long that it is a joy for the cooking smells to connect with my primitive brain and for my body to respond. The aromas tickle my taste buds until they are fairly dancing with expectation. "Get ready. Something good is coming," they trumpet.

Over the next weeks and months, I experiment. I learn secrets. I make chicken noodle soup with homemade noodles, scallions, and lots of mushrooms. The secret to that recipe is adding balsamic vinegar in the last 15 minutes. It provides a difficult-to-distinguish but enticing flavor and the steamy chicken broth soothes my soul.

The secret to thick split pea soup is tarragon. And to chili, it combines soy sauce, worcestershire sauce, and cabernet. Always in spaghetti sauce add dry white wine. And lemon herb dressing makes a terrific marinade for mild white fish. Grilled over mesquite it is "incredible," as my neighbor Ted describes it. I am more verbally discriminating now. I call it succulent with a rich flavor.

Herbs are always rubbed between the palms to release their flavors and it's best to sauté onions a very long time over low heat. I find an intriguing recipe for French onion soup which requires onion rings sautéed by themselves for 15 minutes and then simmered in beef broth for another 35 minutes. Then I add flour. When the broth is thick and bubbly, I heat it for 20 minutes more. Add the cheese and croutons and place it under the broiler for a minute and Ted is knocking on the door to investigate the "yummy" smell. Ted's vocabulary regarding gourmet delights is limited but his enthusiasm isn't. He becomes my taster.

Cooking is an expression of myself and an expression of love. My interest in cooking began because I wanted to take care of Robbie. I am inspired to do more for him than I have ever done for myself. Now my caretaking has grown beyond the kitchen.

Cooking is my way of making a home, sharing my love, and expressing my creativity. I truly can't believe that I can experience all that from an activity I have avoided assiduously for years. When I spend time in the kitchen chopping and blending, I feel part of an encompassing process. I'm not focused on time and I'm not "trying" to cook. I am just doing it. I let my mind go and I am totally attentive to the food I prepare. I am caught up in a swirl of creativity that is taking form in my kitchen. The creativity isn't mine in particular and can be directed into any activity. For me, it just happens to be cooking. Cooking is the context in which I experience moving beyond my mind and my will and joining with something greater than myself. And it all began because of Robbie's need for me to care for him.

The practical part of me likes cooking because I have something tangible in the end. Doing therapy is great but at the end of the day, I sometimes wonder if I had actually accomplished anything. Here I can see and smell and taste what I have done.

I make lots of mistakes, too. A mushroom soup recipe, highly recommended, calls for rosemary. I misread the measurements, inadvertently adding more than twice as much rosemary as the recipe requires. Ted knocks on my door and asks if I have seen Rosemary. "Has she fallen in the soup?" he jokes but doesn't hesitate to take some home.

So, cooking is a way of making relationships — both with Robbie and with my neighbor but also with others. I can now, for the first time in my life, invite anyone over to dinner and not suffer with dread and anxiety. Barry comes and shares my latest culinary trial and his latest paragliding adventure story.

A year ago, I would have envied him and traded my position in the kitchen for his in the sky. But not now. The magic and the partnership I first discovered in the sky I now experience in my kitchen.

Cooking is fun because the act of cooking itself is play. Hannah is teaching me to take all the time the recipe requires and to enjoy each step. There isn't anything to be saved by hurrying and everything can easily be lost by a flame too high or a simmering time too short. Cooking demands my attention and the food reflects the quality of my attention. It is attention that makes a home.

If I move slowly and allow the time that is needed and do so with a loving heart, then the recipe works out well. I need to be gentle with myself and my expectations for what is possible before I start cooking. I want to be interested and willing to spend the time it takes. And I am. Because of Robbie.

Why was it so much easier to make a home for Robbie than it is for me alone? I don't know but I feel a responsibility to provide for him and teach him and protect him. And I will do that, no matter what it takes. How did I become so maternal? A puzzle.

The space in my kitchen and my home became sacred in the same way that the space in the sky had been sacred when I was paragliding. There is an aura of timelessness in both places that precludes tension or fretting. What is going on, in both the sky and in my kitchen, is valuable because, in my most essential humanity, I am participating in the realm of the gods.

I'm not cooking for my own personal gain or glory. I feel called to be in my kitchen and to choose to participate with gentleness in the creation of life for someone other than my adult self. Truly, in this area, I have to acknowledge that anything good that comes isn't from my will. I simply surrender and let myself be pulled. I follow my heart tugs and watch to see what happens.

In both paragliding and cooking, I recognize the sacredness that exists and I respect it. Cooking becomes a holy thing to do. It can also be done quickly and haphazardly and then it leaves me anxious and dissatisfied. But when I let it be important and give it my attention and care, the act of cooking is a celebration.

I learned that that is true for everything I do but I would not have learned that about something which I already took seriously. When I was studying in graduate school, I knew that improving my skills as a therapist was valuable and so I was willing to give that my time but I always had a goal in mind. I was paying attention to my courses when I took them because I wanted to be somewhere else in the future.

I had to learn about true attention with something I hadn't before valued. It isn't the cooking in itself that is holy, it is my attitude towards it that makes it sacred. Hannah tells me to make my home sacred by paying attention to the details. It is my attention that transforms it from an abode to a sanctuary.

And, so, I live attentively and gently and with care. And that attitude softens the space in my home. It welcomes me, Robbie, Ted, and Barry. I have turned into an Earth Mother. I snort in the way Hannah does when I realize that. What a change from my earlier days, driven by worry and self-doubt.

I have to disagree with David. It isn't paragliding that is the most passionate intense experience I can have. It is being me in my home, paying attention to the tiniest details of what I am doing. I notice how Robbie feels. I create a home to express my love and to share my life with him.

Robbie leads me to discover that. His vulnerability and total need for me to protect him touch me in a way I haven't been touched before. I am completely responsible not only for keeping him safe but for nourishing and nurturing him. He is as real to me as any baby any mother has ever held in her arms. His innocence makes me commit to him and his trust inspires me to give more of myself than I had thought possible. I will do for Robbie what I have never done before for myself. Because of him I can be more than I have ever been. Robbie touches a place in my heart that no one has ever touched. I am changed forever.

Being a "mom" is not only creative for me in the kitchen, I allow myself to be involved in a process of creation that is greater than I am. Through Robbie I participate in LIFE. The enormity of that realization overwhelms me. It isn't a project my mind can handle.

But as long as I remain attentive to what is in front of me at the moment, stirring the soup or washing the greens or setting the table, I am carried along. I can't foresee the future; I only live in the moment. And that's what I pay attention to.

Being part of this process of LIFE is ever so much more significant than any achievement or money I have earned. I can't take responsibility for any of it but I feel more satisfied than I ever have. And it is only by surrender that I can participate. By surrendering I have found my heart.

CHAPTER 14
COMING HOME

Robbie, the baby in my heart, grows into Rob, the gentle middle-aged man who comes to dinner. My other figures no longer appear to me in physical form, although I can feel them in me and around me all the time. Sometimes they speak to me through other people. When I overhear a conversation rhapsodizing about the sunset, I surmise it is Maggie telling me to take time and appreciate what is around me. I hear Hannah chortle when grocery store Pete tells me a silly joke. Sometimes Theresa's words come out of the mouth of a stranger. I recognize them as Theresa's because they tug at my heart. Rob is the only one I see and sit with and talk to now. He has changed over the months I have known him and fed him. When he was a child, I gave him my attention and concern about his comfort.

Now that he is an adult he gives me his presence. He sits at my table with his forearms resting on the side of the table and leans as far back as his chair permits. He stretches his long legs under the table, crossing them at his ankles. Sometimes his feet get tangled with mine and he laughs. Rob is always relaxed.

His body is slender, not as thick as Alex's, but not at all fragile.

There is a quality of sufficiency to him. I can feel his self-acceptance and contentment. It's as though he is saying, "This is who I am and I am enough." Very low-key, very unpretentious. He is who he is and that is that.

Rob doesn't say more than he needs to, either. He never tries to impress me or convince me or influence me. He is as accepting of me as he is of himself. Rob's light brown eyes almost match his slightly darker brown, thinning hair. He combs it over the top of his head and to the side; over the months I've known him there is less to comb. This inner world figure ages in the same way that human men age. It's probably my expectations that led me to see that.

Rob is exquisitely sensitive. Alex had been forceful when he spoke to me. When he had an idea, he wanted me to understand, he had been adamant about drilling it into my brain. In contrast, Rob is the best listener I have ever met. No matter what I am rambling about, he cares what I say. He listens to my heart and hears the words I don't speak.

Rob still likes eating with me and, I admit it, my cooking has improved. Our meals have become mini-events. Sometimes he shows up for dinner sporting an ascot. The beautiful silk scarves that he wraps around his throat lend an air of sophistication. He has grown a mustache; some evenings I would describe him as dashing. Dressing up seems to be fun for him.

Rob always compliments me on dinner, being creative to do so at times, as when the soufflé fell or, more precisely, never rose. "Smells divine," he whispers with his eyes closed, considerately not seeing the sad blob of mushy corn on his plate.

Rob offers me a way of experiencing life that I come to realize I need. I haven't felt my Controller since the beginning of this adventure but I think Rob is as different from her as is possible. Everything about Rob bespeaks poetry. He discerns the paradox when I rush home to meditate or when I am frustrated after I have committed to surrender to whatever the day brings. He notices the metaphor of opening on all levels — windows and doors on the physical, opportunities and friendships on the interpersonal, and insights within me. He shows me how what I experience in relationships in the world reflects the relationships among my inner world figures. He discerns the thematic threads running throughout my week and inside me.

His favorite topic of conversation is "Integrity with a capital I."

After so many years of thinking in personal terms when I practiced individual therapy with clients, I was relieved to hear Rob talk about the integrity of life.

"You see, Annie, it's like this. In your case it's not so important what you do; you've done far too much already — getting so many degrees so young, opening an office by yourself, purchasing your home. Now what counts is how open you are. You aren't one little separate individual person who has to think for herself and work to protect herself. Your job is to know your heart and to let it guide you. That's what's been missing. Everything you need you can have if you listen to your heart."

Rob smiles as he leans back and stretches his legs. We have just dined on herbed chicken I baked in a clay pot with green beans seasoned with fennel. Now we drink chai tea.

"Life isn't the struggle you have always expected, Annie. You were the one making things hard, not life. You were the one who said being yourself wasn't OK, that you had to do more and have more and be more, and, whew, you really did it, didn't you?" And he laughs.

Rob tells me I have lived in an off-track way for the first part of my life and by his laugh he tells me that he loves me. Not "even though" I have made some self-sabotaging decisions or "because" of what I did or "in spite of" anything. Rob loves me for being me. Very simply, he knows me and he loves me.

He continues. "And that was fine. You played that craziness out as long as you could. Now you have no doubts about whether or not you're ready to change. Now you're free to fly." He laughs heartily as he throws back his head. Rob can see a vision I can't.

"What's going on, Rob? You know something you're not saying."

"You are in for so much fun!" He grins. "You have all you need now to really enjoy yourself. And I don't mean just letting it rip at parties. How about giggling your way through every day?" I start to laugh, too. His enjoyment is infectious but I really don't know what I am laughing about.

"I want the details, Robster. Give me the bottom line, black and white. What's up?" I feel like a knight who is being sent from the castle on a journey and I'm not sure where I am going or what I will encounter.

"No way, Annie, my sweet. The surprise is the fun. You have your integrity." And he stops abruptly as though a thought has struck him. He continues in a more serious tone.

"Integrity. You know what integrity is, don't you?" I don't need to answer but I want to feel part of this conversation so I reply, "Sure, wholeness."

"Right, wholeness. Oneness. Unity. You are very well acquainted with Hannah and Maggie and Theresa and Alex and me. You know you can call on us whenever you want and that we are committed to you. We have different, um, qualities, shall we say, to offer you, but, really, we are all you. You have integrity inside as long as you are aware of all of us and stay open to hearing from us.

"It's when you block any one of us that you lose your integrity. If you pretend like you're not Theresa's despair, you lose your wholeness. And if you neglect to see Maggie's creativity, you lose some aliveness. You aren't fully you without all of us."

Why is he talking to me like I am a schoolgirl? "I know all that," I answer with an impatient sigh just as a schoolgirl might. "I've been open to everything all of you have told me."

"And that's why you don't see us as individuals anymore. We're inside you. You hear from us without even knowing it. We're part of you. And that's what integrity is." Rob pauses. "On the inside. But the world is bigger than just you, Annie." He looks at me from the corner of his eye. Does he think I will object to that statement?

"Say, it, Rob." His gentleness can be annoying when I am ready to pick up the pace and move on.

"Life has integrity, too, and it's your job, for the rest of your life, to live in that integrity and to find your rhythm in it. No more setting your personal goals and distinguishing yourself. No more trying to stand out. Now it's time to listen and to move as you are directed to move. And not to move if you're not led to do so!"

"So, what are you telling me, Robert?"

"Most importantly I'm telling you to listen. Listen to all of us folks inside. You've gotten that down pretty well and none of us is pressing you to notice a missing piece. So, now listen to your own rhythm. Be silent in the mornings. You don't have to jump up. Take twenty minutes to lie in bed and get a feel for your day.

"Receive. You're being given to all the time. Acknowledge that. Trust it. Your greatest wisdom is in surrendering to how you are led. Don't be too ambitious for yourself. After all, who is the self who is striving? And for heaven's sake, only let your mind do what it's made to do — organize the details of your days, not the days themselves. Let your heart open your days.

"Ask for gifts. Ask for guidance. Don't be afraid to move into every part of you. Don't hide anything in the shadows. Bring it all out and look at it and lick it and chew it up.

"You see, Annie, this is for keeps. Now you're living for real. There isn't any future that's more important than today. This is it. What's here today is what is and you can grab it with Theresa's zest or you can pass. But if you pass and lose it, it's gone. It's your choice, Annie. You have all the help and support you need; we're always right with you and we will be, whatever you do. Life is leading you. It's up to you to follow."

Rob stands and walks to the window seat. He looks into the night with the street light's glow and the passing cars. I look away from his back and pick up my teacup. And when I look back, he is gone.

I haven't seen Rob again since that night but I feel him hold me when I sit in the dark and my mind is still. And I feel him when I call to him just to be with me when I walk through the autumn days with the air chilled around the edges. Fall always reminds me of Rob because that's when I saw him last.

I don't miss him. He's with me. I've just moved on.

I've found that what I do isn't as important as how I do it. Being productive doesn't count for much unless it unfolds naturally and easily. I don't have goals. It doesn't matter where I go if I'm not completely here when I'm here. So today, this minute, and this second are my only concerns.

I'm leaving my future up to life to show me. I'm taking care of today. I've learned what it means to be present to myself and to other people, to have my heart with me and open, to surrender to life and trust and be receptive, to listen to my own rhythm. Moving at my own pace is what my integrity is about. Not trying to fit in or be like someone else or adjusting. I know how to listen and listening is my job. Being still and listening.

And when I listen, I am gently (or sometimes roughly) directed. My guidance is clear after a while if not at the beginning and all I need do is follow it. I don't need to understand it, make sense of it, or be reasonable about it. I just need to trust it.

I don't know where it's taking me but that doesn't matter. I've already gone down a path to a goal. The rest of my life is about surrender and trust. Because that's the most exciting way I can live now. Aligning myself with my own guidance and being me as totally and as joyfully as I can. I really don't have time for anything else.

I've learned that running after success is just another attempt to curtail the creativity of life. I've done success but now I want to do aliveness. So, every day I wake up and, just as Rob suggested, I lie in bed and ask, "What do you want from me today, life?" And I wait and I listen and I receive. Maybe not words or thoughts but I receive whatever it is life wants to give me. And I surrender my day to life and I accept whatever comes in my path.

At the end of the day, I say, "Thank you, life, for showing me what it is to be me and to be alive today." I truly do feel overwhelming gratitude. The mystery is so great and I've been given my own personal communication. A direct line, so to speak. I'm very well taken care of and I'm very very well loved and I don't have to do anything. Just open my heart and surrender to life.

www.ingramcontent.com/pod-product-compliance
Lightning Source LLC
Chambersburg PA
CBHW031441120626
46545CB00006B/2513